Praise for *R*

My heart was touche ... *jor Unbridled Joy*. I found Cathy Wilson's story and insights to be fresh and compelling, a lifeline to those longing for hope when it comes to past shame and discouragement. This book gently opens a window to what's usually shrouded in darkness. The light that shines through is the grace of Jesus Christ and the joyful impact He can make when we give everything over to Him. Cathy points to God as the compassionate Healer, the divine Father, and our Rescuer God who always offers forgiveness, direction, and intervenes when we need Him the most. I would highly recommend this book and encourage you to buy one for a friend today.

Jeff Wallace
Lead Pastor, Hikes Point Christian Church

Tears. So many tears. As I was reading my friend Cathy's book, I shed tears of both heartbreak and sorrow over the many ways that Satan's lies and plans of destruction seemed to roll like waves over her life. Then came tears of praise and, yes, joy, as she shared how the Lord redeemed "what the locusts had eaten" in her life. He took the broken pieces of sin, shame and guilt and created a beautiful masterpiece, through the work of redemption and the power of the Gospel. In this book, Cathy not only bravely shares her story but because she doesn't want to waste her journey, she also shares lessons on post abortion syndrome, parenting, dating, marriage, and ultimately a clear call to those who may still need to put their faith in Jesus.

Moriah Gilbert
Mom of three children and Senior Pastor's wife, Third Avenue Baptist Church

Almost like a modern-day Joseph, Cathy's life has been filled with trials. Yet instead of allowing these to defeat her, she leaned into God and survived. Now she offers amazing help for others who may face similar challenges. Her memoir is packed with Godly wisdom for teens, parents, and women who know the pain of abortion, miscarriage, adoption or who struggle in their marriage. It took great courage for Cathy to share her story, but I am so glad she did. I highly recommend this book to anyone.

Elizabeth Bogard
Friend and former Teaching Leader in Bible Study Fellowship

I have been privileged to walk alongside Cathy as her counselor and spiritual mentor during many years of her life journey. *Rescued for Unbridled Joy* describes Cathy's life, including her unique challenges and her recovery from guilt, shame, and depression. Cathy's memoir showcases the amazing, redeeming love of God poured into her life over many years. Cathy's journey through childhood struggles, adolescent pressures, young adult decisions, and adult demands and influences, will resonate with you, inspire you, and fill you with hope that no matter what experiences and choices are part of your story, God is bigger. Cathy's story is our story. Our choices might not be the same and our struggles may be different, but God is the same God that has written Cathy's story and is writing yours too.

Danna Delafield
Licensed Psychological Associate, KY Center for Anxiety and Related Disorders

It is my pleasure to recommend Cathy's book, *Rescued for Unbridled Joy*. I'm confident that many people (especially women who struggle with guilt after an abortion in their past) will be inspired to receive God's forgiveness and healing because of Cathy's testimony. Cathy's story reminds the reader that although there are ups and downs in the Christian life, the Lord is faithful.

Bob Russell
Retired Senior Minister, Southeast Christian Church

Rescued for Unbridled Joy is the perfect title for this heartfelt story of healing and hope. It is beautiful to see how God lovingly leads us while we travel with Cathy on her journey from the captivity of sin, guilt, shame and depression to freedom in Christ. As she shares her struggles, she brings the wisdom and insight she gleaned over the years and encourages hurting hearts while never failing to point to Christ and the life-transforming truths of the gospel.

Laurie Aker
Executive Director, Thistlebend Ministries

As I read through *Rescued for Unbridled Joy*, I was reminded that Christ followers are often dulled into a sense that those sitting next to them in church are squeaky clean and couldn't possibly have a story of their own sin, shame, and brokenness. Church folk seldom, if ever, learn of these things in our journey together. What if your story resonated with someone suffering in the pew next to you, who needed the chance to say, "You, too? I never knew!" We keep so much buttoned up, but Cathy has woven into her memoir childhood, adolescent, and adult sin and pain, and revealed how her journey with Christ has healed so much. He truly is Savior, Redeemer, and Friend, and not only heals, but strengthens, overcomes, and indeed, gives purpose. This memoir is not just about her, but about you, and how you can and do have the opportunity to also be rescued for joy.

Monica Henderson
Executive Director, BsideU for Life Pregnancy & Life Skills Center

If you only read her resume, you would think that Cathy Wilson was an accomplished, confident woman who made the right decisions for a successful life.

But hidden beneath the surface is a tale of deep pain and misguided choices that could only be redeemed by a great God. Cathy tells the story of her life's journey with a vulnerability and, at times, heart-wrenching honesty that many would recognize in their own lives but few would be willing to tell.

And she fills her book with wisdom gleaned from reflections on Scripture. Though anyone would benefit from Cathy's book, I would especially recommend it to teens and young adults living in a sea of societal dysfunction.

J. Mack Stiles
Director of Messenger Ministries Inc.

Each one of us has a story of how God has pursued us with His love. Cathy's story is filled with ups and downs and a long journey to emotional, physical, and spiritual health. In the introduction she writes, "God prefers to unravel our bondage over time as we come to know, appreciate and absorb His living Word into our very beings." I have found this to be true in my life and the lives of countless others. I encourage you to allow Cathy's story to inspire you, challenge you, and strengthen you on your own life journey.

Joe Donaldson
Director, The Potter's Wheel

RESCUED

FOR UNBRIDLED JOY

2023

Cover image credit: Sharissa Johnson www.sharissajohnson.com

ISBN (Paperback): 979-8-9903303-0-6

ISBN (eBook): 979-8-9903303-1-3

RESCUED

FOR UNBRIDLED JOY

Cathy Wilson

First and foremost, I want to thank the Lord Jesus Christ for saving me and rescuing my life from the pit of despair. Truly, He has turned my mourning into dancing and given me the oil of gladness.

†

I am eternally grateful for the love and devotion of my precious husband, Ralph, without whom my story of redemption would be incomplete. My life has been beautifully blessed because of your unconditional love.

†

I am thankful to God for giving me the blessing of my two children. Stephen and Annika, you have brought me great joy throughout my years of motherhood. It has been an honor and a privilege to be your mom.

†

This book would not have been completed without the encouragement and commitment of my editor and friend, Joanna Sanders. Joanna, you have been a joy and delight to work with. Thanks for having faith in me throughout the writing journey.

†

I am indebted to my many friends for their words of encouragement, prayers, and helpful insights in the process of publishing this book.

CONTENTS

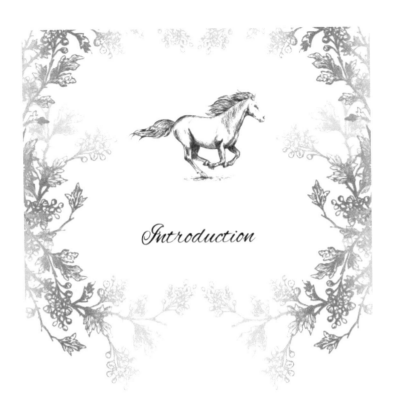

Introduction

My battle with shame began early on and I have fought with it for most of my life. I suppose that I am not the only one who has fought this battle. Many people I have talked with have also had similar struggles. It seems that Satan specializes in leading God's people down the path of feeling ashamed or unworthy of God's unconditional love.

My hope as I write is that others who may read this book will identify their *own* battles with shame and begin the healing process. Healing has not happened quickly for me, but it has taken its own sweet time so that I could appreciate the degrees of healing along my journey to wholeness.

Shame is a feeling that "I am bad," not to be confused with "what I did was bad." It encompasses our identity instead of our behavior. Shame was a cloud of fog that hovered over me for many long years. At times, it buried me in guilt and despair. It relentlessly followed me into my Christian life as well. Surprisingly, God did not immediately take away my deep-rooted shame at the moment when I received His Son Jesus Christ as my Lord and Savior. Perhaps this is because God prefers to unravel our bondage over time as we come to know, appreciate, and absorb His living Word into our very beings.

This book is the story of my personal battles, and the rescue that's taken place at the hand of my God. There are many people involved in my testimony, and to protect their identity I have changed many of the names in my story. Mine is not a neat, tidy story, nor is it a "quick fix" story of how Christianity resolved my insecurity and struggle with shame. It is, though, a wonderful story of God's amazing, extravagant grace poured out on me over the thirty years that I have walked with my Savior Jesus Christ.

Your story may or may not be similar to mine, but if you have ever felt "not good enough" or have been weighed down by overwhelming feelings of guilt or shame, I pray that my story of hope and healing will encourage you in your own spiritual journey. All praise, honor and glory go *to God* for the amazing work that He has done in my life. Truly, He has redeemed and rescued me from the damaging layers of shame and guilt; bringing me into a joy and freedom that I never thought was possible.

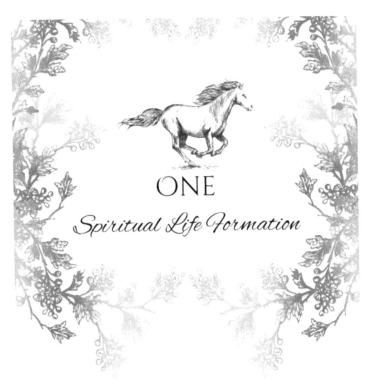

ONE

Spiritual Life Formation

I am the oldest of five children born over a period of eight years. My mom was raised in the Lutheran church and my dad was raised in the Presbyterian church in their respective hometowns. My mom's grandfather was a Lutheran minister, and her parents were both Lutheran. Mom was raised in the Lutheran church in Sunbury, Pennsylvania. Dad was raised by his parents in the Presbyterian church in Olean, New York.

After they were married, they began attending the Presbyterian church together. Mom taught Sunday school for many years while I was growing up. Dad also taught Sunday school and worked with the youth when I was very young. Mom regularly took us to church and Sunday school throughout my childhood and teen years. My paternal grandmother also attended church on a regular basis. My dad and his father were very busy with running the family business and they did not make church attendance as much of a priority. Daddy worked extremely hard Monday through Saturday, so Sunday was the only day of the week for rest or relaxation. Often, there would be golf, work, or other activities which occupied Dad's attention on Sunday mornings.

While my Protestant background and Sunday School teaching included the familiar stories of the Old and New Testaments, there were gaps in my understanding of all the attributes of God and Jesus. My view of God the Father (at that time) was that He was a distant, harsh, and judgmental God. I believed that Jesus was the Son of God who died on the cross to save us from the punishment for sins. I did not know that He is a merciful, compassionate, Savior who forgives and removes sin and gives us His righteousness. The Holy Spirit was known as the Holy Ghost in the Presbyterian faith, and I had little understanding of who He is or what He does.

For whatever reason, the unconditional love and mercy of God was not something I was taught in a meaningful way. I did not realize that a person could have a personal relationship with God or Jesus. Although I did all the "proper" things like attend Sunday school and church, complete the required confirmation class, and join the church, I did not have a personal relationship with God. I did not personalize the fact that it was my own sins that Jesus died for. I did not realize that He shed His own blood *to forgive me* or that I had access to my heavenly Father.

The Holy Spirit was beckoning me to a personal relationship with God just after I joined the church in the eighth grade. I have a vivid memory of sitting in our den trying to read the Bible starting with the book of Genesis. However, my journey through the Bible came to an abrupt end when I got to the book of Numbers! Any Bible teaching I received from then on came through sermons or my participation in the Sunday evening youth fellowship class for teens. Some of you may recall the Good News version of the New Testament. Much of my learning about God came through the pages of this book.

I had a special relationship with one of my Sunday school teachers, Mr. Buckley. He was my teacher during the critical middle school years when

Sunday school started to seem like a burden. Whenever I would come to his class, Mr. Buckley was delighted to see me and just showered me with love and affection like a granddaughter. He made me feel like I was someone special, someone to be cherished. Mr. Buckley always showed me the love of Jesus in his countenance and actions. He was a great Bible teacher too! I respected him greatly, but I did not always pay attention during the teaching time. My mind wandered and I joked and snickered with my good friend Lynn during his class. He might have admonished us once or twice, but never made me feel like I was a disappointment to him. If he were alive, I would love to tell him how much he meant to me. For years beyond middle school, Mr. Buckley was very fond of me and always greeted me with a big "bear" hug. Only in my adulthood as a believer, could I appreciate that God placed him in my life to show me what unconditional love looked like.

Our family prayed before big holiday meals such as Christmas, Thanksgiving, and Easter. My dad would lead us in prayer before we ate and that was the extent of prayer in my family life. While Mom or Dad may have had times when they prayed on their own or together, I never personally heard them praying or talking about prayer. This is not meant as a criticism of my family—simply that I did not come to value prayer as a means of connecting with my heavenly Father. I have often heard it said, "You can't lead others where you have not been yourself."

In high school, I was selected to be a Youth Representative on the Elder Board of our church. At the time, I felt honored to be selected and voted onto this ruling body of the church. I don't think it had anything to do with my spiritual life, but it had to do with my reputation as a young lady with good character qualities and the ability to interact well with adults. Overall, this was a good experience that allowed me to develop some leadership skills and the ability to relate well to adults outside of my family.

My family did as much for me spiritually as was modeled for them. I am especially grateful that my mom made church attendance a priority for this was my introduction to what would later become a strong faith in God.

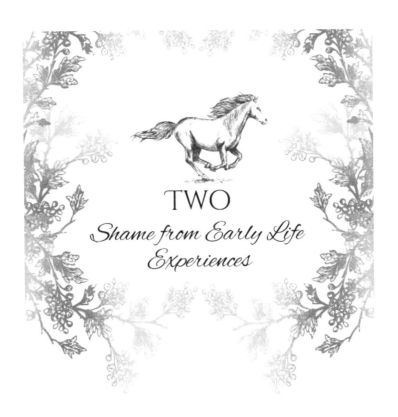

TWO
Shame from Early Life Experiences

I was under the age of six or seven when I first remember feeling the emotion of guilt. I had been playing with a friend in our neighborhood when I told her that her swing set was not really hers, but that it belonged to God because He gave it to her. I vaguely remember our conflict over my blunt statement and remember running home in tears feeling guilty over the hurt I caused her. I do not remember even telling my mom about the incident for fear that she would judge me for my careless words. The friendship was never restored. In fact, there was no effort to reconcile our differences. She never invited me to play again at her home and the friendship was irrevocably broken. At the tender age of six or seven, I did not know how to resolve conflict, much less how to deal with my guilty feelings. From this incident, I believed that when I hurt a friend, there was nowhere to go to deal with my guilt. This experience began my struggle with guilt that did not go away.

A few years later an incident occurred that added another brick of guilt into my heart. I was playing with large rocks out in the circle where we lived. I tossed a rock up high into the air and that rock came crashing down on my sister Judy's head. I remember panicking over what I'd done to hurt her. I felt absolutely horrible and was extremely sorrowful over what I did. Judy screamed out in pain as I tried to comfort her and see if her head was bleeding. It appeared that she was okay and I do not remember if my parents got involved or if Judy even told them. I went to bed that evening afraid that I had somehow damaged her brain permanently. Thankfully, she did not show any sign of brain damage as time went on.

Other than my initial apology, the event was never discussed again. However, I was tortured by the guilt for years to come and was haunted by the memory. Finally, a few years after I became a Christian,

I once again begged Judy to forgive me. Thankfully, she had hardly remembered the incident but more importantly, she expressed immediate forgiveness to me. I was so grateful for her grace and forgiveness, and I prayed that God would forgive me and remove the guilt and shame I'd carried for nearly thirty years. This time, I fully accepted the fact that Jesus had died for this sin of mine.

Another early shame-producing event involved an experience in the sixth grade which I call the "blackboard embarrassment." In the 1960's, it was common for teachers to call students up to the blackboard to work math problems. Although I had been a very good student in all subjects in elementary school, I was stumped by division when it was first introduced to me. My teacher, Mr. Miller, was a kind and gentle man who liked me because I did not fool around in class. I paid attention during class and did my homework assignments in a timely manner. One day, Mr. Miller called me up to the blackboard and asked me to solve a division problem. I recall the heat in my face as I stood there several moments not knowing how to do the problem. I faced the blackboard and did not look out toward the class for what seemed like a long time, perhaps two to three minutes. Finally, I was rescued by another student who was sent to the blackboard to help me. Thankfully, my classmate knew exactly how to solve the problem! However, this one incident caused me to feel very bad about myself and ashamed over my "stupidity." I believe that Satan uses those experiences where we fail to measure up, to make us feel great shame. Oh, how I wish that I had known the grace and mercy of God at that time in my life. Unfortunately, I only knew how to feel embarrassed and disgraced.

When I was twelve or thirteen, I began babysitting for my four younger brothers and sisters. Whenever Dad and Mom went out at night, they left me in charge of my siblings. At the time, I was so relieved to not have a babysitter come to our house that I never stopped to think that this was quite a bit of responsibility for an adolescent. I allowed many games to be played throughout the house, including hide and seek, and a chasing game we nicknamed, "run around the dining room table." I cooked dinner for my siblings—sometimes it was fish sticks and frozen fries. Other times, it was heating canned spaghetti on the stove or baking a pizza in the oven.

One evening, I burned myself while pulling a tray of fish sticks out of the oven and I dropped the aluminum tray on our newly carpeted kitchen floor. I quickly ran to the kitchen sink to put my hand under cold water. It was several minutes before I stooped down to pick up the tray and the fish sticks. Unfortunately, there was a tray-size dark burn spot where the tray had fallen. I was devastated to see that I had spoiled the carpeting and I dreaded telling my parents what had happened. I don't know how someone thought that carpeting in the kitchen was a good idea—but as I remember, the carpeting was replaced with more new carpeting. My parents were disappointed about the accident, but I felt they were more concerned about *the carpet* than my burned hand. I felt extremely guilty over this incident for a long time. Another brick of guilt was added to the load of guilt I was already carrying.

I was never meant to be a cook. I recall burning the canned spaghetti on the bottom of a pan over a burner. This probably occurred more than once because my siblings nicknamed me "Burnie Spaghetti!" At the time, it was funny, but this was the first of many nicknames that I was assigned later in life.

Some of my childhood shame and bad feelings about myself were unintentionally brought on by my parents and grandparents. As a child, I loved horses and daydreamed about having a horse of my own. I read every book about horses that I could get my hands on. Whenever I talked about wanting a horse, the idea would be criticized and squelched by the adults in my family who claimed that my dream was impractical and unrealistic. During one visit to see my grandparents who lived in Pennsylvania, my grandfather took me to a horse farm to learn what was involved in caring for and boarding a horse. The adventure was lots of fun until the car ride home when my grandfather shamed me and criticized me for wanting what was impractical, unaffordable, and unrealistic because we did not live in the country. He went out of his way to "prove" to me that my dream was not going to be realized. I soon learned that my dream was not understood nor was it worthwhile to keep asking my parents for a horse. I remember how sad and withdrawn I was after the lecture by my grandfather. While he may have been well intended, I ended up feeling ashamed of myself because I still wanted to ride, own, or simply be around horses. My dream was crushed but I had no one to share my heartache with. Sometimes adults simply do not understand children's desires and dreams!

I still remember where I was sitting in our family room after watching an episode of the TV show "Lassie" when I was seven or eight. I was crying because of something sad that had happened in the episode. I was told to stop crying or "I'll give you something to cry about!" That expression would be repeated to me over and over again whenever I cried about something that my mom or dad thought should not make me sad. Throughout my childhood, I tried hard not to cry or express the emotion of sadness because I knew I would be reprimanded for crying. I have felt an inordinate amount of shame for being a sensitive child.

There were other experiences in my childhood when guilt was a very *appropriate* response to my sin. I quite vividly recall my attempt to steal a magazine from the local grocery store where my mom had shopped for years. After visiting the public library one Saturday with my sisters, we stopped in the grocery store and headed for the magazine section. As previously mentioned, my love of horses drove many of my thoughts in those days. I'd seen the magazine "Western Horsemen" among the many other magazines in our grocery store and loved to browse through the beautiful photos of horses in the magazine.

On this particular day, I was so strongly attracted to the magazine that I decided to steal it! While my sisters stood guard in the aisle, I slipped a copy of the magazine into my library book bag. As we began to leave the store, however, the manager (who knew my mom and our family quite well), stopped us and asked if we were going to pay for the magazine that he knew was in my book bag. Quite horrified at being caught, I told a lie and then gave the magazine back to the manager. This sinful action caused me to feel extremely guilty for a long, long time. Worse yet, I feared that the store manager would tell my mom what I'd done the next time she visited the store. You can imagine how I felt every time I had to go to the store with Mom—embarrassed and very guilty. For years after, I had to see that manager and know that he never forgot what I did. Nor did I ever forget how ashamed I felt every time I stepped foot into that store. I did not know what to do with my guilt mainly because I did not know that Jesus would forgive me of my sin.

One of the problems I faced was what to do with the guilt I felt on a regular basis. Our family did not regularly express regret for hurts caused and damage done. The words "I am sorry" were not really part of our family's vocabulary. Even worse, the words "I forgive you" were not often spoken by my parents or grandparents, nor were there efforts to make restitution when someone hurt someone else.

What does a young girl do with her guilt and shame over sin? She translates it into "I must be messed up" or "I am a bad person." This is especially true if a child does not realize that God forgives people of sin. And if her parents do not express sorrow over their sin and ask forgiveness, there is no example for the children to follow. Our family had high morals, but there was no regular teaching and training on how to deal with guilt, anger, and hurt, or how to reconcile after a fight or quarrel.

I have now been a Christian for over thirty years, and it has taken me a long time in my walk with the Lord to be able to let go of embarrassing moments or failures. Satan has often won the battle in causing me to feel bad about myself when I've sinned or disappointed those whom I love. But God, in His mercy, has helped me to confess and repent over my sin and to accept His forgiveness through Jesus Christ. God never meant for me to carry the burden of shame over the childhood experiences I have written about.

Through much counseling and prayer over the years, I have been able to thoroughly forgive my parents and grandparents for those things mentioned above. I have even come to see my sensitivity as a gift from God and have learned to accept that God created me to experience all emotions. Thankfully, Satan *has not* won the victory by keeping me in the prison of bitterness toward my family. Today, through the unconditional love of Christ, I have come to believe that I am forgiven and forever set free from shame. Yet, before I got here, there would be many more years of battling ahead.

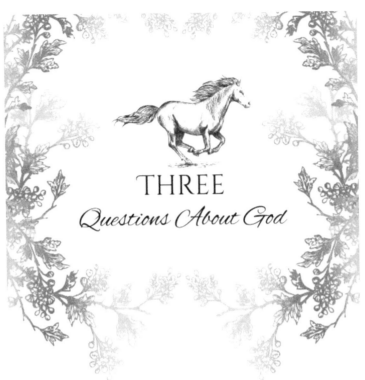

THREE
Questions About God

The first time I remember questioning God and wondering if He even existed was when I experienced the loss of my first piano teacher who was also Mom's best friend. I started piano lessons when I was about six years old and my teacher, Mrs. Pratt, was a very kind and encouraging woman. She always made me feel special and loved. I had been taking lessons from Mrs. Pratt for a couple of years and I was beginning to make real progress. I thrived under her patient teaching style and continual affirmation. She became pregnant with her sixth child while I was taking lessons, and I knew that we would stop lessons for a few weeks when she had her baby. What I did not know during my last lesson before she gave birth, was that I would never see her again. I soon learned that Mrs. Pratt died of complications while giving birth, something I had never heard of happening before then. I was devastated and could hardly believe that I would never see her again. Mom was even more distraught as they had been dear friends for years.

I do not recall asking my mom questions about what happened, nor did she talk openly about her loss at that time. I remember crying and being very sad for my loss as well as Mom's loss of her friend. Other than sharing the news that Mrs. Pratt had died, Mom and I never discussed any details, nor was I given an explanation of why this had happened. It seemed that I was not permitted to talk about my feelings. Perhaps I recognized that Mom was hurting and that it would be hard to talk about the loss, but I did not dare bring up the subject. Whatever the case, in my mind at the time, I could not believe that God would allow a young mom to die and leave six children behind. *What kind of a God would let a mother die while giving birth to her child?* This experience led me to my thought that God was not as good of a God as I'd thought Him to be. If He was truly good, this tragedy would not have happened. Satan would use this lie about God's goodness in my life, for a long time to come.

I had other experiences in my early teen and mid-teen years that caused me great sadness, anger and feelings of abandonment by God. One of those involved the loss of my cat, Tiger. My cat was a surprise gift from Dad and Mom on my eleventh birthday. The year was 1969 and it always stands out because it was on my birthday in July of that same year that United States astronauts walked on the moon! I'd always had a fondness for cats, especially kittens, and it had been a huge blessing to receive my birthday kitty. Tiger followed me everywhere and even though she was friendly with my siblings and my parents, it was *my* lap she'd always land in whenever I was sitting on a sofa or chair. Tiger also jumped on my bed every night and slept next to me. While our home's thermostat was turned down at night, I always remember feeling snuggly warm with my cat sleeping next to me. In a sense, the cat provided unconditional love and comfort when I was distressed or upset about things going on in my life.

About two years later, my family and I were about to make a short car trip to the family cottage on a nearby lake. We'd made the trip many times throughout my life, but on this one occasion, Dad thought it would be nice to take Tiger with us in the car on our way to the cottage. I remembered how much the cat hated car trips to the veterinarian and how wild and upset she was when riding in the car. I told Dad that I thought the cat should stay at home where she would be safe—we'd left the cat behind many other times when we traveled to the cottage for the day. I remember begging Dad to not take Tiger in the car with us, but he insisted that everything would be fine. The ride to the cottage was not a peaceful ride with the cat meowing, almost howling, as she tried to hide under the seats. When we arrived at the cottage, one of my brothers opened the car door and Tiger leaped out of the car, running toward the creek.

I chased after her thinking that she would stop running when she heard me call her name. My cat was never seen again after that fateful car ride. I spent the next two days searching all around the cottage and surrounding property, including the creek bed where Tiger had run away. I remember calling the cat and walking for hours up and down the creek looking for her. Unfortunately, my parents were not available to help me look for Tiger. They were committed to entertaining guests for the Member-Guest golf tournament at the country club. I believe that my grandparents were staying at the cottage with us, but I don't remember that they helped in the search for my cat either.

Because my parents were away most of the weekend, and my grandparents were busy caring for my four siblings, I felt very much alone in my heartache that weekend. I'm certain that Dad and Mom felt badly that the cat had run away, but I don't recall them saying that they were sorry. And I don't recall being allowed to cry with any support or hugs from them or my grandparents. I felt completely alone in my anguish over the loss of my cat and there were no adults to show empathy or to comfort me in this huge loss. Many people may think that the loss of a cat should not be a big deal. But to me, I had lost a precious companion and pet that had meant a great deal to me.

I came to believe the lie that I was not important or that my loss did not matter to God or anyone else who loved me. I now know that God *did care* and that He saw my grief and anguish that weekend as well as into the weeks and months to come. But at the time, I did not know God as my Abba Daddy and I was angry at my biological daddy for taking the cat with us in the car.

I think that not being able to talk about or express tears over this loss was the hardest thing. I was learning to adapt to the unspoken rule that strong expressions of emotion, especially sadness and anger, were not welcomed or encouraged in the course of our family life. Therefore, I had no outlet to deal with the hurt or anger that I felt. I suppose that I thought if God *really* loved me, He would have helped me to find my cat. Satan took advantage of my vulnerability and spiritual immaturity, and this was the beginning of the lies I believed about many things that happened during childhood. My two nagging questions about God were: *"Where was God when it hurt?"* and *"Why did He let me down?"*

Another experience I had that made me question God was when my mom received a phone call that would dramatically impact her life and indirectly affect mine as well. There had been a car-train accident in Addison, New York, where my Aunt Sally (Mom's only sister) was visiting their grandmother at the time. Aunt Sally had been released from a mental hospital for a weekend visit with my grandmother and great-grandmother who lived in Addison. Aunt Sally was being treated for severe post-partum depression after giving birth to her third child. It was felt that she was well enough to be released for a short time under the care of her mother, my grandmother.

While Mom was on the phone with my grandmother, I recall seeing her break into sobs and cry hysterically like I'd never seen her cry before. Apparently, Aunt Sally had slipped away from my great-grandmother's house and walked into the path of an oncoming train near the house. At the time, I was told that it was a car-train accident and that Aunt Sally had been in the car which collided with an oncoming train. It was years later before I would learn the devastating truth that Aunt Sally did not die in the car, but that she had committed suicide by walking into the path of the oncoming train. It was traumatic enough for me to think of a car being hit by a train but imagine how much more upsetting it was to learn the truth about Aunt Sally's death.

After Mom returned from attending Aunt Sally's funeral in Pennsylvania, she was never the same again. She cried often and was very sad for years to come. I now know that she suffered with significant depression after Aunt Sally's death. But we never talked about her grief over the loss of her sister. Even though I had lost my aunt, I knew not to bring up the subject or to ask for any details about the accident. Mom and Dad did not talk about the loss of Aunt Sally in front of us children and we simply understood that this was not a subject to talk about ever again.

I think the secrecy of the accident and not being allowed to grieve openly added to the enormous weight of this loss. While I understand why the adults in my family did not choose to reveal to me the true cause of Aunt Sally's death, what I came to believe once again, was that you did not talk about or cry about sad things that happen in your family. More importantly, this loss in my early life left me once again questioning God's goodness in allowing this accident to occur. You can only imagine how much more I questioned God after learning the truth several years later. I simply could not understand how a loving God would allow such a tragedy to happen. I rejected the notion that even though God was a loving God, accidents happened and hurting people make poor choices. I guess I needed someone to blame for all the pain in my mom's life, and so I blamed God.

Mom also suffered the loss of her brother a few years later when he died of cancer at the age of thirty-two. I accompanied Mom on her last visit to see Uncle Chuck in the hospital before he died. While I thought I was mature enough to handle seeing him, the sight of this once strong man in his frail and weakened state due to radiation really upset me. I was haunted by his devastating appearance for years. He died shortly after our visit and Mom had to bury her remaining sibling. He left behind a wife and two young children. The aftermath of this loss was more than Mom could take. Her depression and grief were magnified in a way that only as an adult could I fully appreciate. As a teenager, though, the loss of Uncle Chuck further strengthened my negative view of God. I actually thought God *was cruel* to allow my mom to lose both her sister and her brother at such young ages. My grandparents' grief over the loss of their son and daughter was enormous and whatever faith in God they had was shaken irrevocably. Their heartache was extremely profound, and it seemed to me that they never got over the loss of both a son and a daughter. Years later, my poor grandfather had a heart attack in the cemetery where he'd been trimming the grass at Aunt Sally and Uncle Chuck's graves. He died at the burial plots of his beloved children.

Needless to say, Mom was devastated again, and my grandmother's heart was forever broken. I was particularly close to my grandmother, and I watched her grieve for the rest of her life. She did not talk often about these losses, but as a teenager, I could only imagine that she was somewhat bitter toward God. I don't know for sure, but I suspect that her relationship with God was profoundly impacted. I continued to question how God could allow so much tragedy in one woman's life. Because I was very close to her throughout high school and college, my grandmother's struggles in life affected me very much.

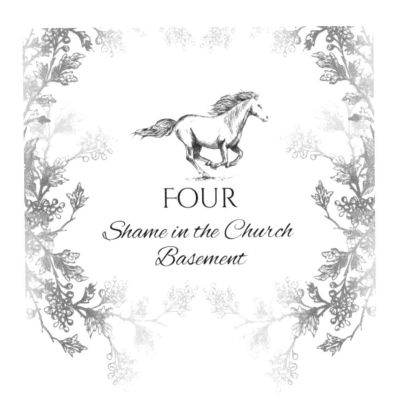

FOUR

Shame in the Church Basement

While writing this chapter, I reflected on a message at church which resonated deeply with me. The sermon focused on the importance of having our vertical relationship with God as the priority in our lives. Only when we look to Jesus, the only true source of unconditional love, can we love and properly relate horizontally to our spouse, family, and friends. The pastor stressed the need to know God and respond to His love before trying to pour love into another person. He specifically encouraged singles to passionately pursue a relationship with Jesus Christ as they are not distracted by many other relationships to manage and others' needs to be met. When we are single, we have the time to wholeheartedly devote ourselves to knowing our Creator and developing intimacy with Him. Reflecting now, on my own years of singleness, I know this time in my own life could have been used more intentionally to seek after God with all my heart. I am so thankful that my teenage children heard this encouraging message about singleness and dating from a Christian perspective.

At the same time, I am profoundly sad that I did not hear such a message early in my life. If I had the Lord Jesus Christ as the foundation of my life back in my teens and twenties, much heartache, brokenness, and shame could have been avoided. Even from my middle school years, shame as it related to relationships with the opposite sex started to take root.

As I mentioned earlier, I was actively involved in our church's youth group from seventh grade through high school. Many happy memories were made with my friends and the special young couple who led the group and mentored us. Some of those memories include Bible teaching from the Good News Bible, roller skating, ice skating, Christmas caroling, choir practice, and weekend retreats. As I recall, we also participated in service projects in our area. The Youth Fellowship group met primarily on Sunday evenings at the church. Often, there would be "free" time in the gymnasium prior to, or after the teaching time. We would play basketball as well as hide and seek in the church basement. Although the group leaders were in the church, they would not necessarily be present to fully chaperone the free time activities.

During the hide and seek games, my friends and I would hide in every imaginable place in the whole church. No closet or room would be off limits except the church office and the pastor's office, primarily because they were locked! One evening, I had chosen to hide in the choir robe closet in the back of the darkened basement. I thought I was well hidden until one of the boys found me hiding among the choir robes in this closet. Of course, there was hilarious laughter and squealing when I was finally discovered.

However, something else was discovered that night, and it was that this boy wanted to kiss me in that dark closet. This was a boy that I liked, and honestly, I was attracted to him and delighted in the fact that he was pursuing me. Surprised and shocked at this new form of attention, I willingly participated in the kissing exchange. While I thought this was just his way of saying that he liked me, he was just doing what an adolescent boy's hormones were urging him to do. I so much wanted to be cherished by someone and I thought this was surely the answer to this strong need of mine.

I wish I could tell you that this was the only occasion that this happened. However, there were many more secret rendezvous in dark closets or stairways throughout the church. I grew to crave the attention I got from this boy as well as others from the youth group. At that time in my life, I did not feel very good about myself because I had acne, red hair, and a rather skinny body. One boy in the youth group once told me that I had a face like a dog, and so he nicknamed me "Duff the Dog" after a popular cartoon at that time. I could only assume that my acne-prone face was the catalyst for this nickname.

I was shy, but the attention made me feel like I was attractive to at least a couple of the boys. Apparently, I was very vulnerable, and naïve. I began to flirt with the boys on Sunday nights and I enjoyed their attention. What I didn't know then, was that teenage boys with raging hormones would not be content long with just kissing. And so, as months passed, they would make sexual advances and demand sexual touching during the brief moments in a closet or back stairway. Apparently, I was so in need of male affirmation and physical affection, that I cooperated with their desire for sexual touching. This is so embarrassing to admit, even now, decades later. At the time, I guess I thought this kind of behavior was normal for teenage boys and girls, and I did not know to flee from sexual immorality as God's Word commands in 1 Corinthians 6:18. I only knew that in the moment, I was made to feel that I was special or wanted by someone. I must have been very spiritually lost during these years or I would have recognized that this fondling was not an expression of true love or devotion. I did not know that my Heavenly Father loved and accepted me unconditionally or that His own love was the answer to my love hunger. Otherwise, I think I would have been hesitant to participate in the sexual exploitations of these boys. I never breathed a word about what was happening to my parents or the youth group leaders. I just thought what was happening was normal in some way. Only decades later would I even consider that these experiences were a form of sexual abuse. But because I *willingly participated*, I could only feel shame, horror, and self-disgust that I'd permitted this immoral and disrespectful treatment to go on.

I only tell this part of my story to communicate especially to my younger readers that any sexual activity outside of marriage is not God's intent or design. His plan is for us to treat our bodies as temples of the Holy Spirit and to flee sexual immorality of any sort, regardless of how close you may feel to a young man or woman (1 Corinthians 6:19). Engaging in sex outside of marriage will eventually leave you emotionally damaged and worse yet, your soul will be "tied" to anyone with whom you have been sexually involved.

It would be great to tell you that I went on to date or go to the prom with one of the boys I had been with in the church basement. The ugly truth is that they never asked me out on a real date. Apparently, I was only good enough for their sexual exploration in the secret places. I was beginning to feel used for their sexual pleasure rather than someone worthy to befriend or date. I felt dirty and rejected, rather than respected or cherished as a daughter of the King. Of course, at that time, I did not even know what it meant to be a daughter of God. I had not had any biblical training at church or home to prepare me for boys and dating according to God's design. These experiences left me spiritually and emotionally broken, and I had nobody to talk to about what had happened. Worse yet, I had to cope with the fact that my girlfriends from the youth group were going on real dates with these young men. That made me feel even more unworthy and rejected. I also became resentful and angry toward the boys. All of this left me unable to form healthy friendships with young men, thinking that physical involvement was going to be expected or demanded. I believed the lie from Satan that my self-worth was dependent on whether or not boys asked me out on dates.

Thankfully, when I was a junior or senior in high school, I was asked out by one or two boys who were friends from the youth group. The feeling of being asked out and not pressured for anything physical left me feeling refreshed and appreciated for who I was. These young men knew nothing of the experiences I had with their peers in the youth group and to this day, I am grateful that I have some recollection of appropriate dating experiences from my high school years. I also dated a few boys from my high school who treated me well and were not interested in kissing or making out! My final date of high school was for the prom in my senior year. This boy was from my church and his parents were acquaintances of my parents. However, this young man was unlike the other boys I knew from the youth group. In fact, we were friends and he had always treated me with respect and kindness. My memory of that prom night is wonderful because of the way he treated me the entire evening despite my inexperience and awkwardness with dancing!

Soon I would be off to college—but my high school experiences with the boys in the youth group would haunt me and follow me into my college years and beyond. God would ultimately forgive me for my sin, and I would eventually forgive the boys who had abused me, but my experience with them left me angry and feeling bad about myself. No matter how much my parents loved me and affirmed me, it did not seem to be enough. They never knew about my secret scars from the church basement. And for decades, nor did anyone else.

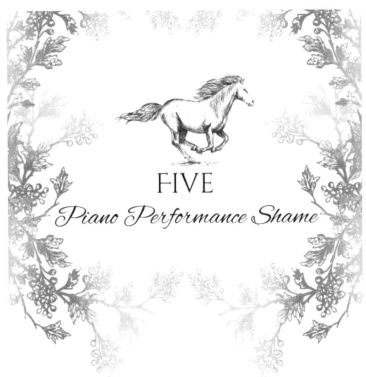

FIVE

Piano Performance Shame

The piano has been a major part of my life since I was a young girl. I began learning to play when I was about six years old. I'm not sure whether it was my own idea or my parents' idea that I would take piano lessons. As I mentioned earlier, I had a very loving and affirming piano teacher as my first teacher. I had about two years of instruction from her before she passed away. It was in the first couple years of lessons that I learned to appreciate and love playing the piano. My mom played our piano at home and I still remember hearing her play her favorite songs, including "White Christmas," "Blue Room," and several Broadway hits. I admired my mom's ability to play the piano and I dreamed of being able to play as well as she did.

After my first teacher died, I began to take lessons from another teacher named Mrs. Hooker. She also loved her piano students and encouraged them to play their pieces perfectly by memory. I progressed well under her teaching and was soon playing intermediate level music before the age of twelve. Mrs. Hooker had two recitals per year for her students to perform primarily for parents and grandparents. While I did play well at most recitals, I almost always experienced significant anxiety and "stage fright" before these events. I was one of the more advanced students she taught, and so my time to play was usually near the end of the recital, as she had her most advanced students play at this time. Very frequently, Mrs. Hooker would compare me to a student who was a year ahead of me in school. Indeed, I heard her play her pieces impeccably in the recitals, never once making a mistake that I could discern. She was a very gifted pianist and I secretly aspired to be as good a musician as she was.

The problem was that whenever Mrs. Hooker bragged about her star student, Danae, I was left feeling that I would never measure up to her ability. I don't think it was ever intended that I would feel badly about myself, but nonetheless, I knew my ability to play would probably never measure up to Danae's natural giftedness. While I worked very hard and was disciplined in my practice time at home, I always sensed that I was being compared to this girl. Whenever I went to county or state solo competitions, I knew that Danae would receive a perfect grade. My teacher always made me aware of how well she had played for the judges. I usually performed well but did not receive perfect scores. I became obsessed with performing at a superior level in every piano playing endeavor. But I knew I would never be able to play as well as she did, no matter how hard I tried. She was naturally talented and always played more advanced pieces than I did. Mrs. Hooker was extremely proud of her students, but she was especially proud of her star pupil's accomplishments. Eventually, I came to believe the lie that my *value* as a person was based on how well I *performed.*

Throughout high school, I played piano for the chorale, the orchestra, and the drama club. I considered these opportunities to be a privilege and I worked hard to be an excellent accompanist. But underneath the surface, I secretly despised myself if I made even a minor mistake that no one else would notice. My mom and my grandmother came to every recital or high school play or choir concert in which I played the piano, but even their best affirmation and praise did not seem to defeat the "less than" attitude I had toward my own ability. Satan was very strategic during my high school years in causing me to feel ashamed of a less than perfect performance. My choir teacher who asked me to accompany the choir was always very quick to praise my performance, but once again, it just did not seem to be enough.

The truth of the matter is that I was continually comparing myself to Danae and was rarely satisfied with my own performance. Today, I can truly accept and believe that *I was good enough* to play for those groups and events or I would not have been repeatedly asked to play. It was not until many years later, that I would acknowledge and admit that I was jealous of Danae. Jealousy is a sin that creates envy, discontentment and eventually bitterness toward God and others.

On a positive note, I ended my high school piano lessons with a solo recital in which I played several difficult pieces completely by memory. The recital was held in my church's choir room (yes, in the church basement!) and was well-attended by family, friends, and high school teachers. After the recital was over, I recall my father telling people he didn't realize that I could play that well! He had listened to me practice through all the years I took lessons. But he did not come to truly appreciate my progress until that senior solo recital! I was very pleased that Daddy was so proud of me, especially since he paid for lessons all those years.

While I am thankful for the classical piano training that I received all those years, I must say that my struggle with perfectionism was very real. After all, the goal of playing music is to play it well and that was my constant pursuit. I think that my life struggle with perfectionism has its roots in my piano playing experiences. However, I am so thankful that God has given me the ability to play the piano, especially for my own enjoyment!

Many people have asked me why I did not major in music in college. I have often regretted that I did not major in music. I suppose that if even one person would have encouraged me to do so, I may well have pursued music education as a major. At the time, however, I thought I was not "good enough" to be a piano major. Although I chose to major in Biology, I continued to take private lessons from piano professors in the music department.

I started lessons with a male professor during the first semester. He was a kind and encouraging teacher who challenged me to play more difficult music than I'd played in high school. After my freshman year, I was assigned to an older, female piano professor who was not very nice and was very demanding. While I spent lots of hours in the practice studios, I was always nervous to go to my lessons with her because I was afraid of her criticism. Whenever I made a mistake of any kind, she would stop my playing by clapping her hands and then making me sit in silence until I figured out what I'd played wrong. Often, it would take me up to a minute to identify what measure or note was incorrect. I would perspire immediately as she stared at me for what felt like an eternity. Often, I would feel humiliated by the end of a lesson. With this teacher, I always felt like I was on the "hot seat" of judgment. Even when I played well, there wasn't more than a nod to communicate her approval. These were very stressful lessons because I felt ashamed when I made mistakes, even very minor mistakes.

Why on earth I put myself through years of studying with this woman, I do not know! There were other teachers available, but I lacked the courage to ask for a different professor. The emotion of fear was something I felt strongly, especially when I was asked to accompany a senior vocal or instrumental major in their senior solo recitals. I was honored to be asked to accompany other students and I actually enjoyed playing for them. I was not intimidated by these challenges even if my critical teacher was in the audience. Interestingly enough, I received "A" grades each semester that I studied with this tough lady! Upon graduation, I completed my years of piano lessons and was happy to be relieved of the stress of constant practice. Since God doesn't waste anything, He would later show me how He could redeem these experiences for His own glory.

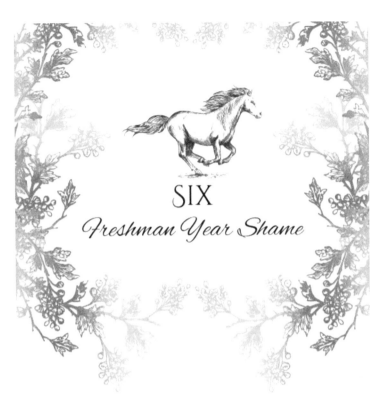

SIX
Freshman Year Shame

I'll never forget the night before I went away to college. Seated at a table with my mom and dad in a nice restaurant, we talked about the new challenges I would face as a freshman in college. We talked about how to handle money, how to approach more difficult academics, and we discussed the option of joining a sorority. What stands out more to me now are the things *we did not talk about.* Dad and Mom graduated from the college I was to enter—Bucknell University, located in the heart of beautiful central Pennsylvania. They had met and dated throughout their college years and so they shared some of their college experiences with me.

We did not talk at all about the drinking and parties which were hosted by all the fraternities on campus. We did not talk about what dating looked like in college, or how to balance free time with studying. I acknowledge that I did not ask them many questions … I was nervous and sad about the prospect of leaving the only home I had known where I'd enjoyed wonderful relationships with my sisters and brothers. In many ways, I was not prepared to face the social and academic challenges that lay ahead.

When I first arrived at college, I cried profusely when my parents left me to drive back home. My intense emotions were a mix of sadness and fear about what was ahead for me. Nowadays, many college freshmen know or at least have met their roommates before starting school. However, back in the late seventies, most freshmen were matched with roommates quite randomly. My roommates were quite different from me in many ways. One of them was outgoing, friendly, and talkative. The other roommate was more introverted yet seemed more mature than the other two of us. She had attended a prep school in New England and had already had the experience of living away from home for two years before college. She was a biology major, and I could tell that she was quite smart. I had chosen to major in biology as well, hoping to pursue a degree in veterinary science upon graduation.

My freshman year began with learning to share a small space with two other young women who studied and slept at different hours than I did. Finding my way around campus and taking advantage of the many activities for incoming freshmen, I began to meet other freshmen who befriended me. While I enjoyed meeting other people, there were a few embarrassing moments that came with introductions. My last name was "Campbell" and I soon learned that there was more than one way to pronounce my last name. I had been raised hearing it pronounced like "camp-bell," as in two different words linked together. However, my new friends questioned me and sometimes laughed when I pronounced my last name in this way. Nearly everyone I met at Bucknell pronounced my name as "Cambull" without vocalizing the "p" in Campbell. At first, I suffered the embarrassment of the quizzical looks and the laughter. Finally, I just gave in and pronounced my name the way other students pronounced it (e.g. the wrong way, as I saw it)!

While weekdays were filled with attending classes, studying, and going to meals with new friends, the weekends were a different story. I found that I had extra time on my hands and needed to begin doing whatever other freshmen did. Some of the freshmen in my dorm had hall parties which featured games, popcorn, and drinking beer. It wasn't long before I was introduced to fraternity parties as the main social scene on campus.

It seemed that fraternity parties were the main way that most freshmen ventured out into the social life on campus, and I was no exception. I had no desire to attend a fraternity party on my own, but my roommate Linda was quite willing to accompany me. What I did not realize at the time was that upper classmen living in frat houses were very welcoming and eager to get to know new freshmen, particularly women. Looking back on my college life, I realize that I was quite naïve when it came to the purpose of these parties. Alcohol of many varieties was served at all the fraternities, but I knew nothing about grain alcohol which was offered to me during one of the first fraternity parties I attended. It looked like Hawaiian Fruit Punch in the large bowl and seemed quite harmless. I first drank the "fruit punch" at the fraternity (Delta Upsilon) where my dad belonged when he was at Bucknell. It tasted good and went down quite smoothly and in fact, it relaxed me enough to have easy conversations with others in attendance at the party, both freshmen, as well as upperclassmen who belonged to the fraternity.

As the evening wore on, I began to feel especially tired and was ready to head back to my dorm. I began to walk on the road which led me back and I found my head spinning as I became very dizzy. At the time, I didn't think much of it, but I later realized that I was *very intoxicated*. I had a difficult time making it to my dorm, but that was not the worst of the effects of the grain alcohol. When I went to bed, I felt that my bed was spinning out of control, and I began to feel nauseous. After a few minutes I felt so sick to my stomach that I began to throw up in my bed. As I got out of bed to get to the toilet, I was so dizzy that I stumbled into the door frame and bumped my head. When I finally reached the toilet, I fell to my knees and began to throw up. Even when I thought I was done throwing up everything in my stomach, the waves of nausea kept coming. I really don't know how long I was on that bathroom floor, but it was a long time. My roommates were awakened by now, and they cleaned up the mess I'd made as well as helped me back into bed. The bed seemed to spin out of control all through the night, but I suppose I managed to sleep some.

I woke the next morning with a splitting headache as I'd never had before. I think I was still somewhat drunk even when I attempted to get out of bed for the day. I do not remember much about that day, but I recall having to wash the white bedspread which had turned as pink as the color of the grain alcohol I had drunk the night before. The bedspread was never white again after this incident! When my parents came for Parents Weekend later in the fall, I'm not sure what my mom said about it, but I don't think I told her the truth about how the white bedspread became so pink!

And so, that is the sad story of how I began to drink and party throughout my days in college. At the time, I thought that was what you did to have fun and meet people. Only years later did I learn that there were many other choices I could have made to engage socially at my college.

Attending men's sporting events was another way I pursued social engagement while I was at Bucknell. My roommates and I especially enjoyed fall football and soccer games played on beautiful, sunny Saturday afternoons. We loved to cheer for one of the freshmen players on the varsity soccer team, as we knew him, and he was always very friendly. We'd met him in the common area between our dorms and had talked with him a few times. George was one of the first male friends I made early in my freshman semester.

After the soccer games, George would come over to where my friends and I were seated to greet us and thank us for coming to the game. George was the star freshman player who usually scored several goals during the games. He did not mind that there were several freshmen girls lined up to congratulate him on the team's win. He seemed to be interested in me and even flirted with me. I was craving male attention at that time in my life, so I enjoyed the teasing and flirtation! My friends seemed to think that he especially liked me. I did not think much of it at the time, but later it seemed that he was interested in getting to know me.

Soon I was attending parties and social events at George's fraternity where we talked and got to know each other better. My roommate and I played a phone prank on him by dialing his phone number and then entering a few extra numbers before quickly hanging up. We had learned that those few extra numbers would produce the sound of a woodpecker pecking when the other person answered their phone. It's hard to believe that the woodpecker calls were so fun to make, but we soon were receiving the same calls to our room.

Our friendship gradually became more than a friendship and it seemed that George considered me more as his girlfriend than just a friend. The relationship progressed more quickly than was appropriate until one evening I found myself alone with him in his dorm room. Exchanging a few kisses led to a situation that I had not anticipated. He pressured me to have sex with him, and for a number of reasons I finally gave in. One of the poor reasons I yielded was because I thought he would dump me if I did not have sex with him. Unfortunately, I was a very needy young woman who was willing to do anything to keep the only serious boyfriend I'd ever had. This turned out to be one of the worst mistakes I ever made in my life, because there were a multitude of repercussions. I had believed the lie that I would remain his girlfriend if only I gave in to his pressure to have sex.

From the moment I left the dorm room that night, I felt dirty and ashamed that I had surrendered my virginity to this young man. I don't know if he felt any embarrassment or not, but the relationship ended abruptly after that evening without any explanation or communication. I was left alone to think about how foolish I'd been. Worse yet, my feelings of worthlessness and rejection deepened when I discovered that George was pursuing the roommate I was not close to. The final blow was inflicted the night he came to our dorm room to pick up my roommate to take her to his fraternity's formal dinner dance. I'll never forget the hurt and anger I felt toward him for dumping me without even telling me why. This first experience of boyfriend rejection would be repeated in my life with even greater consequences to come.

I shared very little about how this relationship ended with anyone who knew me well. I chose not to confide in my sisters, mother, or friends because I was embarrassed and feared their judgment. I wish I could tell you that I learned my lesson from the short-lived relationship with George. However, that is not the case, but I will spare you the details of the rest of my "dating" experience at college. I believed that since I'd lost my virginity, there was no "starting over," so it did not matter what choices I made in the future. Although nothing could be further from the truth, Satan had gained a foothold in my mind and in my belief system. I could not imagine that God still loved me and was willing to forgive me for my immorality. Only years later would I learn the truth about my Heavenly Father's great love and mercy toward me.

After I became a Christian, I found a verse in my Bible which said:

If only you had paid attention to My commands, your peace would have been like a river, your well-being like the waves of the sea.

Isaiah 48:18

This verse is so true. I would have enjoyed significantly more peace in my life if I had known and obeyed God's commands back in my teens and twenties.

Some of you can relate very personally to my experiences. You may even have been married for years, but you still carry the weight of sexual sin prior to your marriage. Others of you have hopefully avoided the choices I made and are experiencing peace in your relationship with God and others. Still others of you are reading this book and realizing that you are on the path of sexual immorality, and you want to jump off that path immediately! Many women and men are in hiding and are experiencing much shame and guilt, the consequences of sexual involvement outside of marriage.

The good news is that there is a *Redeemer* whose name is Jesus Christ. He desires for all of us to experience His amazing grace and forgiveness for those things of which we are now ashamed. If you repent of your sin, Christ will wipe your slate of sin clean and restore you. Because of His mercy displayed in His death on the cross, our sin is forgiven, and our sin debt is paid. You can enjoy an abundant life filled with God's peace and His presence when you know and accept His forgiveness. "There is therefore now no condemnation for those who are in Christ Jesus" (Romans 8:1, ESV).

If you are not yet married and you are having sex with your boyfriend or girlfriend, you can have a fresh start with God. If your boyfriend truly loves and respects you, he will understand your position of not wanting to have sex prior to marriage. Similarly, if your girlfriend is committed to you, she will be willing to respect your desire to postpone sex until you are married. When you repent of sexual immorality, God will forgive you, help you to avoid giving in to sexual temptation, and He will give you a fresh start.

I realize that we live in an age where sexual immorality is rampant and is encouraged by the culture we live in. The world tells you "If it feels good, do it" and that it is fine to have sex with someone who is not your spouse. However, God's Word in 1 Corinthians 6:18-20 commands us to:

Flee from sexual immorality. All other sins a person commits are outside the body, but whoever sins sexually, sins against their own body. Do you not know that your bodies are temples of the Holy Spirit, who is in you, whom you have received from God? You are not your own; you were bought at a price. Therefore, honor God with your bodies.

Remember friends, it is never too late to ask for God's forgiveness and to experience His life-changing mercy and redemption!

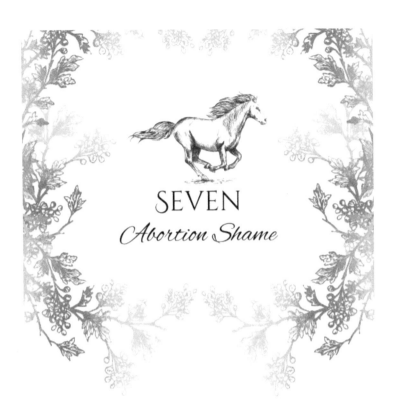

SEVEN

Abortion Shame

When I was twenty-three years old, my sexual sin caught up with me and I found myself pregnant by a man several years older than myself. I was just two years into my professional career with a Fortune 500 company, and I was deeply afraid to tell my parents that I was pregnant. After all, Dad had paid for my college education, and I was expected to support myself and climb the career ladder. While I was never told this was the expectation, I knew that my parents and grandparents would think it devastating to "interrupt" my career to have a baby.

I had a good job and I knew I risked losing the opportunity to advance in my career.

Scared to death, I told no one close to me who could have helped me in this unexpected crisis. I was too afraid of disappointing my parents and sisters, and I was afraid of being judged by both family and friends. In desperation, I finally told another woman I worked with. She could tell that I was devastated and frightened and she told me she knew of an "option" for this unplanned pregnancy.

With trembling and fear, I went to see the doctor she recommended and learned that I could have an abortion to end the pregnancy. I still was unwilling to consult with anyone who could have helped me to realize what I was about to do—take the life of my innocent baby. And so, out of great fear, anguish, and selfishness, I chose to have an abortion. This was the worst possible decision I could have made, though I did not know it at the time. Between my co-worker's encouragement and my boyfriend's growing apathy, I felt I had no choice but to have an abortion.

The abortion clinic did not present me with any information about abortion or fetal development and there was no counseling available about the possibility of adoption. I did not understand that life truly begins at conception. Still, I take full responsibility for making the choice to end my baby's life. At the time, I thought I was aborting a clump of tissue that had not formed into a baby. Somehow, I justified that because it was not yet a baby, that it wasn't wrong to end my pregnancy. I had no idea of the emotional, psychological, or spiritual aftermath of having an abortion. The term "post-abortion trauma" was not even identified or talked about in the early 1980's. Today, it is understood that post-abortion trauma is a form of PTSD (post-traumatic stress disorder). There has been much medical and psychological research to support this finding. Many publications have been written on this topic. You will find several of these helpful resources listed at the end of this book.

I had my abortion on a weekday morning prior to my second shift job at the manufacturing plant where I worked. I recall being very frightened and anxious about the procedure, but the nurses and doctor told me to expect only minor cramping as in my menstrual period. I was asked to relax and lay still on the abortion table as they began the procedure.

The pain I experienced as they dilated my cervix to perform the abortion was excruciating. I will never forget the terror I felt and the complete lack of compassion on the part of the doctor and the nurse assisting the doctor. The sound of the suction/vacuum machine was very loud, and the pain intensified as the procedure continued. When it was finally over, I was covered with a sheet and left alone for what seemed like an eternity. I do not even remember what was more prevalent, the physical or emotional pain.

A few hours later at home, I continued to cramp and bleed heavily, but I was determined to go to work. After all the trauma I'd been through that morning, all I could think about was how I'd explain having to miss work. And I decided that I'd better go to work rather than create a lie about my absence. It is sickening to me now that I tried to carry on as if this were a normal day—going in to work my twelve-hour shift as a Quality Assurance Supervisor, acting as if nothing was wrong.

In the days and weeks that followed, I began to feel a sense of relief that I was no longer pregnant. I thought that my problem was solved and that I could march on with life, never looking back at that fateful day.

However, although I convinced myself that everything was fine, I was not okay on the inside. I worked longer and longer hours to push down the emotional pain—namely guilt and shame. I continued to party after second shift with the managers with whom I worked. My boyfriend was fired shortly after my abortion, and he moved south to find another job. We never talked about the baby I'd aborted or how I was feeling about that decision. The relationship ended without any reference to the fact that it was really *our baby* that I'd aborted.

Years later, I was angry at him for his role in my choice to have an abortion. He did not try to question me or discuss options other than abortion. His passivity and lack of influence in my decision only heightened my anxiety about my pregnancy. In retrospect, I sincerely wish that he, (or any other person), would have tried to talk me *out* of the abortion. I might have listened, but I don't know for sure.

Unfortunately, at that time in my life I did not know God, nor did I realize that God would forgive me for having an abortion. I was in complete spiritual darkness and did not have any desire to seek God or His forgiveness. I was in complete denial that my abortion would have an immense emotional, spiritual, and psychological impact on me for years to come. Denying the fact that I had taken the life of my baby kept me from experiencing the grief that a mother would naturally feel upon the loss of a child.

Little did I know that many years later God had in store for me His great mercy, forgiveness, and abundant life in his Son Jesus Christ. That encounter with Jesus would have a transforming difference in my life.

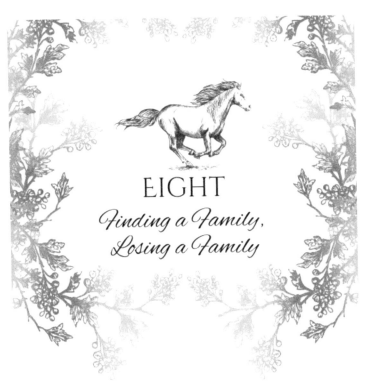

EIGHT

Finding a Family, Losing a Family

A few months after my abortion, God brought a wonderful and handsome young man into my life. One of the other managers I worked with, Mark, had a twin brother who lived about an hour away in the Pocono Mountains of Pennsylvania. I was invited to go snow skiing with him, his brother, and a several other managers from the manufacturing plant where I worked. We met at the ski resort, and we enjoyed a fun day of skiing and getting to know one another while riding up the mountain on the ski lifts.

After the fun day of skiing, I decided to invite Mark's brother, Mike, to attend an upcoming management dinner with me. I was excited that he agreed to go with me. On the evening of the dinner, Mike picked me up in his black sports car! I recall little about the evening except that I thought he was kind, funny, and respectful in every way. The only other thing I remember is that one of the other managers spilled their red wine and it permanently spotted my new cream-colored dress! It was an enjoyable evening otherwise and I hoped that there would be future dates. I had the opportunity to get to know Mike further on more skiing "dates." On occasion, Mike would come to visit with his brother, and I was invited to family meals with Mark, Mike, and their family. Since I was single, I really appreciated being included in these family meals where I got to know and love Mark's wife and children. Mike and I began to see each other regularly when he was in town, and I found that I enjoyed his companionship.

Not long after we were dating, my supervisor at Frito-Lay asked me if I would be interested in interviewing for a Quality Assurance position in another facility. While I was interested in the promotion, there was a huge red flag—this position would be across the country in Denver, Colorado! I had just found a nice young man who liked me and now I was being asked to consider a possible move far away from Pennsylvania. I was torn about what to do. After discussing it with Mike, who encouraged me to at least go for the interview, I decided that I should consider this opportunity.

Shortly after my interview, I received the job offer which I accepted after much inner turmoil. Little did I know that Mike was considering a move to Denver to continue his career as a physical therapist and to continue to date me. I was so delighted when I learned that he chose to "follow" me to Colorado. We each had our own apartment on opposite sides of the city due to the location of his new job.

We both worked a lot of hours during the week and spent most of our time together on the weekends. In the winter, we traveled to the mountains to ski at many of the well-known ski resorts. In the summer, we also spent time in the mountains sight-seeing and hiking trails. Our relationship deepened over the two years we spent in Colorado. Everything in my life was going well when I was offered another job opportunity—this time in Louisville, Kentucky. The only thing I really knew about Kentucky was that it was home to the famous horse race, The Kentucky Derby. Again, I was perplexed about what to do, but I decided to fly to Louisville for the interview. One good thing about a potential move to Kentucky was that I would be closer to my biological family. However, I did not know whether Mike would be willing to move to Kentucky to continue to date me. Our relationship was going well but there were no plans to get married at that time.

My interview went well, and I enjoyed meeting the other managers with whom I'd be working. I was offered the Quality Assurance Manager job which would be a promotion and an increase in salary and management responsibility. I wished that they had not offered me this job because it meant I would have to make another difficult decision. However, Mike seemed very flexible and was open to moving to Kentucky. This move would also place him within a five-hour drive to his parents' home in Ohio. He seemed very willing to pick up again and follow me to Kentucky and so I accepted the job offer. I moved to Louisville before he did because getting a job was not as easy as he thought. He finally got a job as a physical therapist for a hospital about fifty minutes south of Louisville. We both bought townhomes not far from one another and continued to date.

The years that followed were somewhat of a blur. We both worked long hours and some weekends, making it a bit more challenging to spend time together. Year after year passed without a marriage proposal and I was beginning to be frustrated that Mike could not seem to make a commitment. We loved each other very much and were each other's best friend, but something blocked Mike's ability to make a firm commitment to marry. I am somewhat embarrassed today that I spent so many years dating him without moving forward. At that time in my life, my own family was torn apart by my parents' divorce and alcoholism, but I became very close to Mike's family. His parents treated me like a daughter, always welcoming me into their home and making me feel very loved. I now realize that I was emotionally broken-hearted about my mom's losing battle with alcohol and my parents' divorce. The love and acceptance I felt from Mike and his family was very comforting in a time when my own family was being torn apart. Mike's family provided stability and a refuge from the storms raging in my own family.

During those years, I was attending a Catholic church in Louisville with Mike and with his parents when we were visiting in Ohio. I remember thinking, if only I become Catholic, Mike would surely marry me! I actually began the catechism classes before we left Colorado, and I completed the classes upon my arrival in Kentucky. I joined the Catholic faith, convinced that this would be the turning point in our relationship.

Joining the Catholic church seemed like a good decision since I was already worshipping in the church, and I wanted to be a member. However, my hope that Mike would surely marry me if I became Catholic, never became a reality. Finally, after dating for eight and a half years, Mike decided to move to Charlotte, North Carolina, to be closer to his twin brother and his family. Our relationship was struggling partially due to my anger toward him for failing to commit to marriage. We had a few sessions with a counselor, but that did not seem to motivate Mike to move forward.

On the day that he left, I was completely in despair like I'd never been before in my life. Although I had seen the "writing on the wall," I cried and cried for days, barely able to go to work and function. I had lost my best friend, my companion, and my recreation partner. I also lost my connection with Mike's family, the family who had "adopted" me and loved me dearly for years. I felt a deep sense of rejection and even shame because I'd wasted so many years invested in a relationship that did not work out. I even thought that Mike had rejected me because I'd told him about my abortion. The most significant conclusion I reached was that "I was not good enough." I failed to measure up to Mike's standards, thus I felt that *I was* a failure. Satan used that lie to hurt me for several years, even after I became a believer.

I have asked myself often why I completely invested myself in a relationship that was not leading to marriage. I guess I tricked myself into believing that *eventually* we would be married. I lacked enough self-esteem to give up and move on. I was also emotionally needy, and I had depended on the constancy of this relationship to satisfy my deep emotional needs. Another part of me was quite stubborn. I could not bring myself to give up and initiate the break-up myself.

For months after our break-up, I grieved intensely and fell into a deep depression. I was embarrassed to tell my friends and family that this relationship did not work out. I did not know it at the time, but God would use this season of darkness, hopelessness, and despair to draw me to Himself.

I have come to realize now that I had a deep need for a family who would cherish and accept me. After my parents' divorce and the sale of my childhood home, my craving for a family intensified. I had an unmet need for a sense of belonging and a home—a place where I could feel secure and be loved unconditionally. I did not realize it at the time, but I was looking to Mike and his family to "complete" me. Although I was attending church regularly, I did not know I was deeply loved by the One who created me.

I did not know that my Heavenly Father loved me with a perfect and unfailing love. I did not know that He wanted to adopt me into His forever family.

I also now realize that looking to Mike and his family to fulfill me, was a form of idolatry. An idol is anything or any person that you love more than you love God. While I believed in and knew *about God*, I did not seek to know or love Him in an intentional, personal way. Unknowingly, I had allowed Mike and his family to become a "golden calf" in my life (see Exodus Chapter 32). I was placing them first in my heart and mind instead of pursuing God as the priority of my life. Just as the Israelites worshipped a golden calf instead of the one true God, I had committed my own version of idolatry in making Mike and his family the priority in my life.

In Matthew 22:37-39, Jesus declared, "Love the Lord your God with all your heart and with all your soul and with all your mind. This is the first and greatest commandment. And the second is like it: Love your neighbor as yourself." At that time in my life, I was directing all of my love toward a person instead of the one true God.

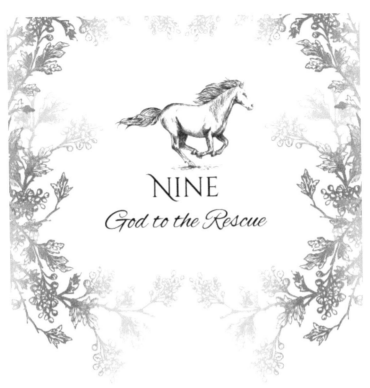

NINE

God to the Rescue

Several months of grieving and self-examination followed the conclusion of "the Mike years." There were two attempts to reconcile and restore the relationship with Mike, both of which were in person. Whenever I felt extremely lonely and hopeless about my life, I would reach out to Mike by phone in a desperate search for comfort. Even though we both still loved and missed each other very much, there was no effort on Mike's part to continue to contact me. Finally, I reached a point when I knew that I needed to try to move on in my life without Mike and his family. However, I still grieved deeply and felt that I was both emotionally and spiritually bankrupt at this low point in my life.

I began listening to a local Christian radio station and found I was comforted by the inspirational music and practical Bible teaching programs. After listening to a talk show called "People to People" for many weeks, I began to think about my own wrongdoing (sin) over the course of my life. I began to see that I was a very selfish person who insisted on having her way about various things. I admitted to God and myself that my sins of promiscuity, abortion, and many other sins were an offense to a Holy God. I began to feel convicted of the sins I'd committed against lots of people throughout my lifetime—my parents, my siblings, friends, boyfriends, etc. But most of all, I was ashamed about how I had disappointed God and resisted turning to Him in repentance and humility.

While listening to "People to People" one evening, I got down on my knees and confessed my many sins to God and asked Him to forgive me. Up to this point, I had not understood what it meant to repent, nor did I really understand that Jesus had died for *my sins.* I now believed that Jesus Christ died on the cross to take the punishment that I deserved. I will never understand the mystery of God allowing His only

Son Jesus to die to atone for my (our) sins. I prayed to receive Jesus as my Lord and Savior and for the first time in my life, I believed that God would be merciful to forgive me.

In the book of Romans, it says, "if you confess with your mouth that Jesus is Lord and believe in your heart that God raised Him from the dead, you will be saved" (Romans 10:9, ESV). That evening was the beginning of a whole new way of life for me. I did not know exactly what had happened to me, but the Bible describes it as being born again spiritually. I realized that I was truly spiritually bankrupt apart from a relationship with Jesus Christ. Just as Jesus said to Nicodemus, in John Chapter 3, "You must be born again," I too, needed a spiritual rebirth. When a person turns to God in repentance and invites Jesus to be their Savior, the Holy Spirit comes to indwell them. I became a new person with new values, new priorities, and the biggest blessing of all, I would one day experience eternal life in Heaven. Just knowing that *all* my sins were forgiven relieved me of the heavy burden of guilt and shame that I'd carried for many years. God had rescued me from slavery to sin, guilt, self-condemnation, and a lifetime of shame! Romans 5:8 (NASB) says, "But God demonstrates His own love toward us, in that while we were yet sinners, Christ died for us."

About this same time, God brought a new friend, Kathy, into my life. I met her at a sorority alumni function, and we became good friends. She soon invited me to attend her church, Southeast Christian church. The first Sunday I attended, she met me there and we sat together. This was very important to me since I had never been in a huge church where thousands of worshippers were gathered. I immediately loved the joyful worship music and powerful Bible teaching. This was unlike anything I'd ever experienced in church, and I was eager to return the next Sunday.

And I did return, Sunday after Sunday without ever looking back. My new friend invited me to attend her adult Bible fellowship class where I made several new friends, *including* the man who would eventually become my husband, Ralph. After getting to know him for a few weeks, Ralph invited me to accompany him to a wedding and I said yes. However, I called him later and told him I him I could not go with him because of a relationship I'd been in for a few months. Yes, there was another young man I dated but we were temporarily "taking a break." I knew I should have told Ralph, "no," in the first place and I was completely embarrassed to call to decline his invitation. Thankfully, he did not hold that against me.

Soon I would officially end things with the young man I'd been dating. I continued to attend the fellowship class at church and enjoyed the kind and gentle way that Ralph interacted with me. I was attracted to him because he was a genuine, committed Christian and he seemed to take an interest in me. In July, I decided to ask Ralph if he would like to walk with me in a city run/walk called "Night Moves." The name of the event may have sounded suggestive, but it was nothing more than a wholesome family event that would take place after dark in downtown Louisville. The night of the walk we conversed easily and had a nice evening together. Soon after the evening of the walk, Ralph invited me to dinner at a local restaurant known for its BBQ. I'll never forget that dinner because in the middle of our meal, the restaurant's fire alarm sounded, and we had to quickly evacuate. It turned out to be a small kitchen fire that was quickly extinguished, and we returned inside to finish our meal. I have often teased Ralph about the "hot date" we had that evening!

We continued to date throughout that summer and developed a close friendship. Ralph took me to meet his parents who lived about fifty minutes from Louisville in the small town of Salem, Indiana. I recall them being very friendly, kind, and sincerely interested in getting to know me. Ralph and I would attend church on Sunday mornings and then drive to meet his parents in Indiana for lunch.

In the fall of that same year, Ralph invited me to attend a PGA golf championship with him. It was a beautiful and wonderful day. We enjoyed walking around the golf course and watched many well-known golfers finish their games at the last tee. Ralph held my hand for the first time that day and I knew that he really liked me. That was a good thing, because I was becoming very fond of him as well!

I was a new Christian, and I was reading an old Bible from my youth Sunday school days. Ralph noticed it was an older translation of the Bible and he promptly bought and presented me with a modern-day translation of the Bible with my name engraved on the front cover. I received this gift with great pleasure and have cherished this Bible for all the years I've used it. Many of our dates during the work week consisted of attending the church's Wednesday night service called "Celebration." It was a time of uplifting singing and practical Bible teaching that was meaningful to me. Somehow, I thought the preacher was speaking just to me on matters I needed to hear or learn about. I found it fascinating to learn so much more about the Bible than I ever did in previous churches.

In the spring of 1992, Ralph invited me to meet him for lunch at the same nice restaurant he took me to after we first met. He also told me that our time together would include a "field trip." I had no idea what he had in mind, but I certainly trusted him and was eager to go. I always looked forward to meeting Ralph downtown on a weekday, but I knew something was up with the field trip. I love surprises, so I looked forward to seeing Ralph that day. Just after we ordered our meals, Ralph asked me if I would marry him, and he pulled out a beautiful engagement ring from the pocket of his suit jacket! I immediately accepted his proposal and he placed the diamond ring on my finger. The field trip was to go to the jewelry store to have the ring sized to fit my finger. Wow—that was the best field trip I'd ever taken! I was ecstatic with joy that I was going to marry this wonderful man I'd been dating for several months. Finally, God led me to the man of *His choice* to be my soulmate and companion for life. My dream of being married was finally going to come true. God had not only rescued me from the shame of my past; He had brought me a godly husband to love and cherish me for the rest of my life. I never thought I deserved a godly man, but God saw beyond my failures and gave me Ralph.

However, there was a hurdle for me to cross before I could marry Ralph. I knew that he deserved to know that I'd had an abortion in my early twenties. I decided to tell him one evening when I was completing a paper for my master's degree. He was with me in an office where I worked part-time, and he was serving as my "editor." As usual, I'd waited until the last minute to finish the paper, so I was quite stressed about that, and was nervous to have to tell my awful secret to the man I would soon marry. When I told Ralph in tears, he told me he was sorry I'd been through that experience and that in no way did he hold it against me. Ralph showed me the same tender mercy that my Heavenly Father had shown me. While I wept tears of shame and regret, he held me and reminded me that God had forgiven me completely. Ralph showed me grace and much compassion when I confessed to him. I told him that my abortion may affect my ability to have children, but even that did not turn Ralph's heart against me. God gave me the strength to tell the one person I so hated to disappoint, and He gave Ralph the grace to love me as He would.

When I admitted my prior abortion to Ralph and he did not condemn or judge me, I realized that there was another secret I had kept from Ralph. Soon after, I revealed to him that I'd had a DUI conviction during the years I was dating Mike. This was also a great embarrassment to me and a source of shame and humiliation. I confessed to Ralph that I spent a night in jail because of my prior arrest for drunk driving. I explained to him what had happened and confessed that I had lost my driver's license and now had a DUI conviction on my driving record. Once he understood the circumstances that led to my arrest, he was not angry at me, nor did he harshly judge me. I told him that I was at a business function where I consumed too much wine and too little food which is a prescription for trouble when driving a car. The consequences of that event were absolutely humiliating, but they did, however, constitute a wake-up call for me. Alcohol abuse was not a path I wanted to walk, especially considering the history of alcoholism in my family.

The weeks passed quickly, and they were a whirlwind of preparation for a July wedding. My mom lived ten hours away, so she was somewhat limited in the help she could provide. She came to Louisville to help me look for a wedding dress. We found just the right one, elegant and tasteful, at a local wedding boutique. Mom was so kind to pay for my wedding dress and help me with invitations. My dad graciously gave us a check that would cover most of the wedding cost. We decided to have a simple yet lovely ceremony at our church followed by a reception at a beautiful horse farm nearby. We were to be married on July fourth, and thankfully, our senior pastor was available to perform the ceremony. There were a lot of arrangements to be made in a short amount of time, but it seemed that God blessed us with His provision and favor in each decision that we made. Our church provided a wedding coordinator who helped us tremendously in planning our wedding ceremony. We had honored God in our courtship, and we wanted our wedding to honor and bring glory to God.

TEN

Surprised by Grace

Ralph and I were married on July 4, 1992 with our families and many close friends surrounding us. I was thirty-three years old and Ralph had just celebrated his thirty-eighth birthday. God blessed us with a beautiful sunny day with low humidity and a temperature in the low eighties. This was highly unusual for a July day in Kentucky. We spent our first night as a married couple at a five-star hotel in downtown Louisville. The next morning, we boarded an early morning flight to Hawaii for our honeymoon. The scenery and weather were very beautiful in Hawaii, and we enjoyed many activities including horseback riding on the beach, hiking, snorkeling, and just relaxing. During that week, Ralph had to make a major career decision about remaining at his current employer (a major hospital and insurance business) or to go with the new insurance business that was going to split off from the original company. God led Ralph to the decision to stay with the insurance side of the business.

The early years of our marriage were very challenging due to various family issues, both past and present. We were very blessed to have friendships with several older couples who modeled Christ-centered marriage to us through words of counsel and the example of their marriages. We also worked with a Christian counselor who helped us overcome many of the challenges we faced. However, I was struggling with depression in these early years of our marriage. Ralph was very supportive, and he encouraged me to seek professional help. I was diagnosed with major depressive disorder and was encouraged to take medication and pursue individual counseling. I did not want to take medication at first, but I chose to follow the doctor's recommendation and between counseling and the medication, I experienced much improvement in my symptoms.

During our early years of marriage, we enjoyed many activities together including biking, hiking, and camping. We also had the opportunity to take trips to different states for vacation. We developed special friendships with other couples who attended our church and often did fun things with these couples. However, my battle with depression lingered on despite being treated with medication. At the time, I did not realize that one of the contributing factors to my depression was my unresolved guilt and emotional distress from my earlier abortion. It was not until a close friend told me about post-abortion syndrome that I began to consider the possibility that my depression might be related to my abortion. As I began to read and learn about how abortions affect women, I realized that I was experiencing many of the symptoms associated with what is called Post Abortion trauma, a form of PTSD. My friend urged me to seek counsel from a local crisis pregnancy resource center, but I was hesitant to do this probably because I was afraid to confront my emotional pain and face the consequences of my abortion decision.

But God arranged an unusual set of circumstances and "coincidences" to get my attention. Specifically, I began "running into" the director of the local crisis pregnancy center, A Woman's Choice. Whether it was at church in the sanctuary or the parking lot, I would encounter Becky, the director, and stop to greet her or talk for a few minutes. It seemed unusual that I kept running into her over a period of several weeks, but I now know that these "chance" encounters were God's plan to lead me to visit the crisis pregnancy center in person. Finally, I made an appointment to meet with Becky to talk about volunteer opportunities at the center. At the time, I thought maybe God wanted me to volunteer as counselor for women in crisis pregnancies. At one point during my interview with Becky, she asked if I'd ever had an abortion. I was honest and told her the truth of my abortion. She asked me if I would be willing to participate in a Bible study designed to help women heal from their past abortions. The Bible study was called "Songs of Deliverance."

What happened next was a moment that I will never forget. Becky showed me the Post Abortion Bible study workbook and when I saw the cover of the workbook, I immediately began to cry uncontrollably. Both the Bible verse on the cover and the picture of what looked like a fortress were penetrating my heart, mind, and soul. You see, I had felt trapped and felt I was captive for years in a fortress or prison with the emotional pain and shame over my abortion. The Bible verse on the cover was "The name of the Lord is a strong tower; the righteous runs into it and is safe"

(Proverbs 18:10, NASB). God *knew* that I needed to run to Jesus with my post-abortion pain to take refuge in Him. I immediately told Becky that I wanted and needed to participate in this Bible study. I realized at that moment that God led me to the center not to become a volunteer, but to experience God's healing for my own abortion pain and shame.

What happened over the next few months was nothing short of a miracle of God. The Bible study was emotionally intense and my former coping mechanisms were no longer available to keep me from feeling the depth of my emotional pain. I began the Bible study with one other participant and a loving facilitator during the weeks just prior to Christmas. This was difficult because I began the process of confessing and grieving over my sin of abortion at the time of the year when I usually experienced the joyful anticipation of celebrating Christ's birth. However, this Christmas found me sobbing frequently in anguish over the loss of my baby and the magnitude of my sin. While the Bible study was full of verses about God's mercy and grace, I felt a profound sense of remorse and loss. My struggle with depression was heightened by the raw emotions I was feeling as I dealt with my abortion wound truly for the first time. It helped me so much to have the other participant experiencing the same thoughts and regrets that I felt so deeply. We were able to encourage and pray for one another as we traveled this difficult journey to healing. The Bible study led me into a season of repentance as well as sorrow over my abortion. This was important as I'd never truly repented specifically over my abortion and had never allowed myself to grieve the loss of my child and the opportunity to be a mother.

Throughout the twelve weeks of the study, there were many verses from the Bible (especially from the books of Psalms and Isaiah) that came alive to me in a very personal way. As I repented and grieved, God spoke new promises of hope and encouragement into my broken soul. These verses became very meaningful and comforting to me and they still encourage me as I think about how God has removed my shame.

Instead of your shame you will receive a double portion, and instead of disgrace you will rejoice in your inheritance. And so you will inherit a double portion in your land, and everlasting joy will be yours.

Isaiah 61:7

Do not be afraid; you will not be put to shame. Do not fear disgrace; you will not be humiliated. You will forget the shame of your youth and remember no more the reproach of your widowhood.

Isaiah 54:4

Set me free from my prison, that I may praise Your name. Then the righteous will gather about me because of Your goodness to me.

Psalm 142:7

Those the Lord has rescued will return. They will enter Zion with singing; everlasting joy will crown their heads. Gladness and joy will overtake them, and sorrow and sighing will flee away.

Isaiah 51:11

He brought them out of darkness and the deepest gloom and broke away their chains.

Psalm 107:14

... for all have sinned and fall short of the glory of God, and all are justified freely by His grace through the redemption that came by Christ Jesus.

Romans 3:23-24

God showed me that Jesus's death on the cross was the punishment for my sin and that there was nothing I could do to earn His grace. As I soaked in the truth about who God says I am, Jesus enabled me to stop punishing myself with self-loathing, and instead, accept His free offer of mercy and forgiveness. Finally, I came to the realization that I was redeemed as described in Ephesians 1:7-8, "In Him we have redemption through His blood, the forgiveness of sins, in accordance with the riches of God's grace that He lavished on us." When I accepted the reality of my redemption, I wept with joy and sang songs of praise to my Creator.

At the conclusion of the "Songs of Deliverance" study, I had the opportunity to choose a name for my baby. The purpose of naming an aborted baby is to give honor and dignity to this child. Although I did not know for sure the sex of my baby, I felt she may have been a girl and so I named her "Sarah." The name of my aunt who died in her early thirties was Sarah and it seemed fitting that just as my Aunt Sally died way too young, so too my baby died when she was at the beginning of her life. What I now know and firmly believe is that life truly begins at conception.

My husband Ralph stood faithfully by my side throughout my post-abortion healing journey. He prayed for me continually and held me when I needed to cry. God has used Ralph's unconditional love for me to help heal me of the abortion shame I had carried for over seventeen years. No longer captive by shame and guilt, I began to experience the truth expressed in Isaiah 61:10:

I delight greatly in the Lord; my soul rejoices in my God. For He has clothed me with garments of salvation and arrayed me in a robe of His righteousness ...

God set me free from the prison of shame I had lived in for so many years. I was now able to live a life free of the chains of guilt and self-condemnation because of what my Redeemer did for me. I am eternally grateful that God led me to this particular Bible study where I confronted and defeated the lies of Satan which threatened to destroy my life.

In the months and years that followed, God continued to pour out His extravagant mercy and grace as I followed His leading to share my testimony of healing in public settings. Shortly after I had completed "Songs of Deliverance," I was asked to share my testimony for a "Right to Life" fundraising walk in a local park. Although I was scared to do this, my dear friend Janet prayed over me and placed her hand on my back the entire time I was speaking. Apparently, a local newspaper reporter was in the audience and when he approached me, I wanted to run away and hide. He wanted to ask me a few questions that would help him write a short article for the newspaper. This was terribly frightening because if I agreed to the interview, the story of my abortion would possibly be read by many other people, including my husband's co-workers. Ralph was completely gracious about this prospect, and I went ahead with allowing the reporter to interview me. His article was published in the local newspaper and my story was just a small part of the article. There were a few people who commented to me about the article, but the comments were positive and affirmed my decision to share publicly.

Later, I was asked to share the story of my abortion healing on the steps of the Jefferson County courthouse during a "Right to Life" rally in mid-January. Once again, I was afraid to speak about my abortion in front of all the people who would attend this event. But as I prayed about the request, I knew that it was Satan himself who was trying to discourage and defeat me. He knew that I was vulnerable to shame and that I hated public speaking. However, many friends prayed for me, and I agreed to share my testimony of God's faithfulness to heal my abortion wound. Several staff members from A Woman's Choice were present to support me. Once again, God enabled me to speak of my abortion and my journey to receive God's healing for my guilt and shame. Every time I shared my testimony, I felt God's affirmation that this was His will for me.

A few years later, I was asked by one of the pastors in my church if he could interview me during a Wednesday night service at our church. I thought that would be okay until I realized that he wanted to interview me on stage in front of the congregation! I was intimidated and just plain scared to talk about my abortion in my own church. There were many friends and people who did not know this was part of my background. Shame was starting to rear its ugly head again and I began to doubt whether I should do this or not. However, I felt that if *even one* woman could benefit from hearing my story, then I was willing to share it with my church family. Ralph graciously gave me his full support, so I agreed to do the interview.

When the day came for the interview, I was very fearful about sharing my story. Many people were praying for me, and God's grace was evident throughout the interview. I was able to remain calm and speak clearly (even though I was shaking on the inside) to talk about my post-abortion pain and how I came to receive God's complete forgiveness for this burden. I emphasized the importance of repentance and expressing godly sorrow for my sin of abortion. After the service, a woman I did not know approached me as I left the sanctuary. With tears in her eyes, she told me that, "my story was her story" and that she was suffering great guilt and shame as a result of her abortion. As she poured her heart out to me, I was able to encourage her to seek post-abortion counseling and to participate in the Songs of Deliverance Bible study. I later found out that her encounter with me led her to seek and receive God's healing and mercy. The Holy Spirit had worked in her heart in a powerful way that evening. I knew that God had answered my prayer that at least one woman would hear and be led to healing, as a result of my sharing. Not only was I was surprised by God's amazing grace toward me that evening, I was also thrilled to know that this woman would be seeking healing for her abortion wound. Amazing grace!

Our Wedding, July 4, 1992

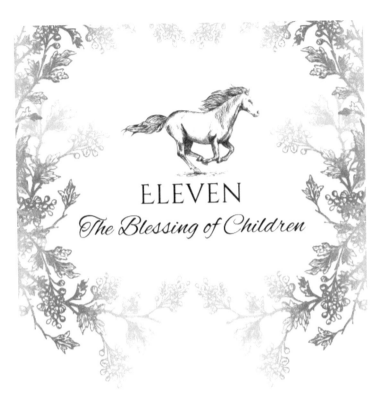

ELEVEN

The Blessing of Children

Ralph and I desired very much to have children, however, it was six years into our marriage before we intentionally tried to conceive. By then we had worked through nearly all of the issues and challenges we faced during the early years of our marriage. By then, my depression was under control, and we were doing well as a couple.

Unexpectedly, in 1998, we lost Ralph's dad and that was a very difficult time. He had battled pneumonia previously, but this time he suffered fatal complications from a drug interaction that caused multiple organ failure. Ralph's mom was having mental health issues that resulted in us devoting a lot of time caring for her as a deeply grieving widow.

At this time, we realized that my biological clock was ticking loudly, and it was time to seriously pursue having children. We were unable to conceive after a couple years of trying and we decided to meet with an infertility specialist. After meeting with the doctor, he gave me the diagnosis of "unexplained infertility." We were told that it was likely that I had a shortage of viable eggs needed for fertilization. We were also told that I had a less than a five percent chance of conceiving and that we were not good candidates for any treatment options. Needless to say, we left the physician's office totally devastated with the seeming hopeless situation. After many tears and much prayer, we decided to seek a second opinion from another infertility specialist in the Louisville area.

We met with this doctor and although he agreed that my chances of conceiving were very low, he agreed to pursue treatment for one or two months. Several tests were involved prior to starting treatment, but nothing remarkable was discovered as the reason for our infertility. He was willing to treat me with a drug that stimulates the ovaries to release eggs. I gave myself the injections and after six weeks, we met with the doctor once again. An ultrasound was performed, and we were elated to receive the news: "You are pregnant!" Ralph and I were totally shocked and amazed at this wonderful news. We *knew* that God had performed a miracle in allowing me to get pregnant after only one month of treatment. I shall never forget the joy we had in telling family and a few close friends later that day. Yes, it was very early in my pregnancy, but we could not wait to tell at least a few people this good news. Many people had been praying for us and we wanted them to know that God had answered their prayers for us. A Bible verse that became very meaningful to me was Psalm 118:15:

Shouts of joy and victory resound in the tents of the righteous: "The Lord's right hand has done mighty things!"

Indeed, the Lord had accomplished a miracle, and we gave God all the glory for our blessing. Apart from some typical morning sickness for a few weeks, I felt very well throughout my pregnancy and was able to continue my routine of lap swimming right up until our baby was born.

We welcomed our son Stephen into the world on June 2, 2000. Due to having a C-Section, I was able to stay in the hospital an extra day to recover and learn to feed our little baby. I was unable to breastfeed Stephen because I was taking anti-depression medication. Although this was a slight disappointment, I believed that it was God's will that I stay on the medication which had helped me greatly. Many people asked me why I was not breastfeeding my baby and in some way, I was ashamed to admit that I needed the medication. I was grateful when people quit asking me the question!

Neither Ralph nor I had been around babies very much, but learning to feed and care for Stephen was a time of great joy. He was a very content baby and easy to soothe even when he cried for short periods of time. My precious husband handled most of the nighttime feedings and diaper changes during the early hours of the morning. This allowed me to rest well enough to handle the daytime routine of caring for a newborn.

Right at the time of Stephen's birth (the day I came home from the hospital), we learned the devastating news that my mom had been diagnosed with Stage four brain cancer. She chose to have radiation treatments immediately, so she was in no position to travel to Louisville to help me care for Stephen. Ralph's mother lived just fifty minutes away, however she had been diagnosed with Alzheimer's disease, and certainly was unable to come to help us with Stephen.

God provided a wonderful Christian lady, "Miss Charlotte," to come to our home for a few hours twice a week to allow me to go grocery shopping and exercise without having to take Stephen with me. Charlotte loved Stephen as if he were her own child, and she cared for him and did light housework as time permitted. Her presence in our home also allowed me to serve in post-abortion ministry at the pregnancy resource center.

About a year after Stephen's birth, we conceived another miracle baby with the help of the fertility treatment. Once again, I got pregnant after just one month of taking the shots to help my ovaries release eggs. We could hardly believe that God allowed us to conceive again—this time I was forty-three years old! Psalm 77:14 says, "You are the God who performs miracles; You display Your power among the peoples." We thanked the Lord for this second miracle and soon told many people we knew that we were expecting.

Just a few weeks into my pregnancy, I had an ultrasound during a routine doctor appointment, and we learned that our baby had no heartbeat. We were completely heartbroken and wondered why God would allow me to conceive a second time only to let our baby die within just a few weeks. We both grieved deeply as we processed this tragic news. I had to have a D & C the very next day and I recall sobbing uncontrollably at this turn of events.

Ralph did his best to console and comfort me, but he was in a state of grief as well. I cried out to God daily, but my grief and depression continued for several months. I took the loss of our second child very hard and although I cried out to God for comfort, my heart remained broken and unable to be consoled. Finally, the Lord revealed to Ralph that he should contact a minister friend of ours to come to the house to pray with us. When our friend Joe came to visit us a few nights later, we described my seeming inability to overcome my grief and heartache. I poured my heart out to Joe, as he listened and responded with great compassion. He opened his Bible to 2 Samuel 12 and read to us the account of King David's grief over the death of the son he had with Bathsheba. In verse 16 of this passage, David pleaded with God for the child and fasted and spent the nights lying on the ground.

When the elders of David's household begged him to get up from the ground, he refused and would not eat any food. When the child died, he got up from the ground to worship and take food again. Listen to what David's servants said to him in 2 Samuel 12:21-23:

His servants asked him, "Why are you acting this way? While the child was alive, you fasted and wept, but now that the child is dead, you get up and eat!" He answered, "While the child was still alive, I fasted and wept. I thought, 'Who knows? The Lord may be gracious to me and let the child live.' But now that he is dead, why should I go on fasting? Can I bring him back again? I will go to him, but he will not return to me."

Joe reminded me that one day, I would be reunited with my child in Heaven. Changing my focus from grieving and weeping, I began to imagine the joy of seeing my child once again and a sense of unexplained peace came over me. Knowing that I would go to Heaven and be with my child there seemed to help me let go of my anger toward God. While this was a process, Joe's ministering to us that evening was indeed a turning point for me. How good of the Lord to send a minister who had previously spoken God's Word over my hurting soul. I confessed my anger and disappointment with God and asked Him to forgive me and restore to me the joy of my salvation.

When Stephen was about four years old, God began to speak to my heart about adoption as a means of growing our family. I believe that God had already been planting the seeds of adoption in Ralph's heart—he became interested in the plight of the young, orphaned girls in China, and he began researching the process of adopting from China without me knowing about it. We attended a couple of adoption fairs where we learned about international adoption, but I was still not convinced that this was God's will for us. Quite selfishly, I was unsure as to whether I could love an adopted baby as much as I loved Stephen. I had many fears and excuses for why I was not ready to explore the adoption option.

During that time, I had the opportunity to participate in a mission trip with my church to Guatemala. It was a medical and dental trip during which God opened my eyes and my heart more to adoption. I served alongside a dentist who was cleaning children's teeth. Many of the children's teeth were severely decayed, or missing, presumably from drinking lots of cola drinks and not brushing their teeth. These precious children were so grateful to us for cleaning their teeth. Most of them came in bare feet because they owned no shoes or sandals. While I can't fully explain what took place on the trip, I only know that God helped me to see that I could have been happy to adopt any one of the beautiful young children we cared for at the clinic. I believe that during the

Guatemala mission trip, God was indeed softening my heart to the idea of adoption.

A few weeks after returning from the trip, I began serving as a children's leader in Bible Study Fellowship, an international study where people in cities all over the world were studying the same Bible lesson each week. I had been a participant and a discussion group leader in Bible Study Fellowship for many years but becoming a leader for children seemed to be quite a new challenge. I was intimidated by all the responsibilities of leading children, yet I knew that if God was calling me to this new role, that He would equip and empower me to serve in this program.

During the first week of the BSF study, I met the children who were placed in my group of two and three-year old boys and girls. I was delighted to learn that an adopted girl from Guatemala would be part of my class. This little girl reminded me of the precious Guatemalan children I had recently cared for as a dental assistant for the dentist on our mission trip. The other children in my group were wonderful, but Sophie was especially dear to me. Finally, my heart was opening to adopting a little girl! God had done the miracle of changing my heart to believe that I certainly *could* love an adopted child as much as I loved Stephen. I truly was open to and leaning toward adoption from either Guatemala or China. My dear husband had a preference for adopting a little girl from China. We were both praying often and seeking the Lord's will for us about which country to adopt a child from.

One evening near the end of that year, we were invited to have dinner with some friends who had recently adopted a Chinese girl. They told us the entire story of their adoption journey while we watched them interact with their new daughter! My eyes were moist with tears as they shared how God had led them to adopt after having four biological children. Ralph and I both listened with excitement and joy when they told us how God had led them to adopt their beautiful little girl. Our friends showed us the photos from their trip to China and told us of how God was faithful to them at every step in their adoption process. I came home from that evening convinced that God was potentially leading us to adopt from China.

In the spring of 2004, we had the opportunity to attend a Steven Curtis Chapman adoption event called "Show Hope" in Columbus, Ohio. During this event, Steven Curtis and his wife Mary Beth shared their story about the adoption of their three daughters from China. In addition, they shared information about the needs of Chinese orphans and the work they were doing to financially support multiple Care Centers in

China. The Chapmans brought their recently adopted daughter Maria on the stage as they talked about the mission of the non-profit organization called Show Hope. Steven Curtis Chapman was one of my favorite contemporary Christian artists and I was thrilled to hear him sing his songs which I'd heard on the radio for years. But what was even more thrilling was that we both felt this event was God's way of helping us to know which country to adopt from. It was as if God was giving us confirmation to pursue adopting a little girl from China.

After the Show Hope event, both Ralph and I agreed to initiate the adoption process which included lots of paperwork to submit to our chosen adoption agency, A Helping Hand, located in Lexington, Kentucky. One of the tasks we needed to complete was a written biography of each of our lives. We knew that I needed to openly admit my battle with chronic depression and the fact that I'd had a DUI conviction many years before I became a Christian. I was so afraid that one or the other of these background issues might be a stumbling block to being approved to become an adoptive parent. I had to get a letter from my psychiatrist certifying that my depression was under control and effectively managed with medication.

Our adoption agency felt that as long as these issues were explained thoroughly, there would not be a problem with the Chinese officials who reviewed our adoption application. The only other concern in our adoption process was the fact that my fingerprints were not clear enough in the three attempts we made to get them done. We then had to write to every state I'd lived in to get a police report that showed no record of crimes! While this was a hassle at the time, the required reports were received finally, and we could move on without clear fingerprints for me.

Ralph took the lead on the application process and was very helpful in moving things along as quickly as possible. We were able to complete the application process and submit everything to A Helping Hand in July of 2004. The adoption agency reviewed the paperwork and shortly after submitted our dossier to the Chinese government. And so began the waiting period of about ten months before we heard that we were approved and matched with our little girl!

While we were considering several different names for our Chinese daughter, the story of Anna in the Bible kept coming to mind. In Luke 2:23-38, we learn that the prophetess Anna was married for seven years and became a widow until she was eighty-four years old. During all that time, she made the best of her years by worshiping, praising, and honoring God. He gave her grace to fast and pray until the coming of the baby Jesus Christ into the world. What this story means to me is that age is of no consequence to God—He can use us at any age. The fact that I would be forty-six years old when we adopted our daughter meant that God had a good plan despite my age! I did not need to worry about being too old to become a mother to a second child.

A little girl in Stephen's preschool class was named Annika and although the name Anna was still foremost in our minds, we fell in love with the name Annika. It is considered a derivative of Anna, and it was an unusual name. We finally agreed that Annika would be the given name for our daughter.

The long-awaited day came in the month of May 2005! We received notification from A Helping Hand that our application was approved by the Chinese Adoption Affairs office. We had been matched with a girl who was fifteen months old, living in an orphanage in the province of Guandong, China. Completely overwhelmed with joy, we praised God and made plans to travel to Lexington that same afternoon to see the photo of our daughter and learn of when we would travel to China.

When we arrived in Lexington at A Helping Hand's office, we met several other couples who had also received their approval notification that same morning. After a few moments of briefing about what would happen next, each couple was presented with a packet containing the photo of the girl selected for us to adopt. I shall never forget the thrill of opening the packet and seeing the photo of our beautiful Annika. There were shouts and tears of joy among all the families who were in the room with us. Our God was faithful to complete the good work He had begun to grow our family.

We considered whether Stephen would go with us on the trip to China. There were pros and cons to having him accompany us on the long flights. We eventually agreed that he should take part in this momentous experience in our family life. God provided our dear friend Lynn to travel with us to help care for Stephen while we were bonding with our new daughter.

When we arrived in China, we were greeted by the woman who would be our escort for the next few days. We traveled by van to the White Swan Hotel in Beijing. This hotel was known for its genuine hospitality to families who traveled to adopt their children. After a night of much needed rest, our escort took us to visit a nearby pearl "factory" where many of us purchased beautiful pearl necklaces and other jewelry made of blue pearls.

The happiest day of our trip was the day that Annika was placed in our arms. Nothing could compare with the joy we felt when we met her for the first time! Her hair was in braided pigtails (which I soon realized were extensions), and she was wearing an outfit meant for a baby boy. We passed her around for Lynn, Ralph, and Stephen to have a chance to hold her. She seemed timid but she did not cry. I cannot begin to describe how wonderful it was to know that this precious girl was our daughter. After completing the required paperwork, we were given a chance to talk with the orphanage director and the nannies who had cared for all of our babies at the Social Welfare Institute in Huazou City. We asked many questions through an interpreter to learn all we could about what life was like for the girls, many of whom had been institutionalized since birth. We learned from their nannies what they had been eating and drinking in the orphanage. We asked about any specific words they had begun to speak and about their bathroom habits. Although the babies arrived in diapers, most of them were accustomed to being placed on very small toilets at regular intervals throughout the day. And therefore, some of the older babies were partially potty-trained.

It was interesting to see which nannies had cared for each baby. It was obvious to see that the nannies were indeed attached to these babies.

After interviewing the nannies, we traveled by van back to the White Swan Hotel to get acquainted with our little girl. Annika was able to pull herself up and take a few wobbly steps. We had arranged ahead of time to take Annika the next day to be evaluated by a Western doctor because her head circumference was reported to be extremely small. We had consulted with a pediatrician in Cincinnati before we traveled to China. We were advised by that doctor that Annika might be cognitively impaired because of malnourishment. We wanted to have an American doctor in China evaluate her physical abilities and cognitive development since she was so malnourished. At seventeen months of age, she barely weighed seventeen pounds. American babies are eating regular food at that age, and Annika had been drinking only formula through a bottle. Regardless of the doctor's evaluation, this precious girl was truly a gift to us from God. We were very thankful to have Annika's medical condition checked by the doctor so we could better understand any specific needs she might have.

We learned from the doctor that while her physical development was delayed, it did not appear that she had any cognitive or other issues due to being malnourished. Annika's very small head circumference was simply a function of not having had proper nourishment.

Once again, we thanked and praised our mighty God for His protection and provision for Annika's life thus far. We returned to our hotel and shared the good report with the other adopting families who were elated with us. Through that experience we learned (once again) that God could be trusted no matter what fearful or worrisome circumstances arose. Psalm 20:7 says, "Some trust in chariots and some in horses, but we trust in the name of the Lord our God." We believed that God is the only One who is worthy of all our trust and that our hopes and dreams were under His sovereign control. Our dream of having a second child to love was coming true!

The entire rest of our time in China was delightful in every way. Although it was extremely hot with temperatures well over one hundred degrees, we always had enough water, hats, and umbrellas to shade us from the sun. Stephen had the hardest time adjusting to the heat—his face was red every time we were outdoors (which was almost every day)! During our stay in China, we were given the opportunity to visit Annika's orphanage several hours away. We decided that Ralph would stay behind with Stephen and Annika, and that Lynn and I would be the ones to make the six-hour trip to visit The Social Welfare Institute in Huazou City. We saw amazing views of the countryside, including mountains as well as flat fields in which people were working in the rice paddies. When we arrived at the orphanage, we were greeted by the orphanage director who spoke fairly good English. We were given a limited tour of the facility where our babies had been raised thus far. When I saw the room in which Annika lived, including the crib she had shared with another little girl, I wept for the little girl who remained there. The cribs themselves were quite a stark contrast to the cribs we use for our babies in America. There was absolutely no bedding or even a mattress in any of the cribs. The babies slept on a piece of hard, white plastic board with no toys or stuffed animals whatsoever. We later learned that the plastic boards were much easier to clean than soiled or wet bedding. Imagine sleeping night after night on a cold, hard piece of plastic!

It was very hot in the orphanage despite the presence of several air conditioning units. There were bugs flying around the orphanage and most of the babies and toddlers we saw were itching multiple bug bites on their bodies. We saw the "nannies" caring for the babies, but it appeared that the ratio of nannies to babies was very low. Another surprise was the rows of lined up portable potties in the baby rooms. Except for the youngest of babies, there was no use of diapers! Those who could sit with assistance were placed on the miniature toilets several times a day so that they could be potty-trained at very young ages.

Very few of the babies or toddlers were crying while we visited the orphanage. We later realized that they had probably learned that crying did not result in prompt, if any, attention from the small number of nannies assigned to care for so many babies. While it was sad to see how our daughter had spent the first seventeen months of her life, we were so thankful that God had provided for Annika until we came to adopt her into our family.

Annika's Homecoming, July 2005

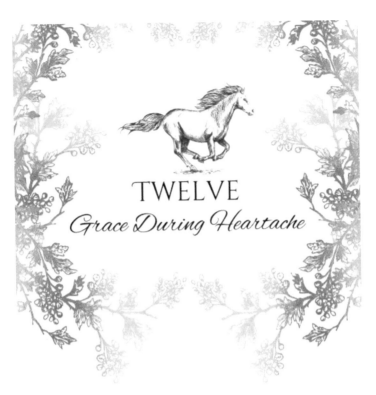

TWELVE
Grace During Heartache

One of the most difficult times in our marriage was when we lost three of our four parents within two-and-a-half years. Our first loss was Ralph's dad, Morris, who lived to eighty-two years of age. He had at least two bouts of pneumonia prior to the one that ultimately caused his death. After enduring and recovering from open heart surgery, Ralph's dad came down with serious pneumonia just a few months after his heart surgery. He was hospitalized and treated with several medications and seemed to be stabilizing. During his hospitalization, Ralph's mom stayed with us for several days but was running out of one of her own medications. One morning, I went to the hospital to stay with Morris while Ralph took his mom back to her hometown to get her prescriptions refilled. However, in the short time that they were gone, Morris began to experience multiple organ failure and the doctors were trying different things to save him. I called Ralph to tell him that things were not looking good, but he was about fifty minutes away. By the time he got back to the hospital, Ralph was shocked to see that his dad was failing rapidly. Within a couple hours, he passed from this life into eternal rest with his Savior Jesus Christ. This was extremely devastating because he had recovered before from serious illnesses, and we had thought he would recover from this bout of pneumonia as well. Only by God's grace did we manage to get through the next days and months following this major loss. Although Ralph grieved terribly, our Lord was faithful to comfort Ralph and prepare him for the task of caring for his mom during her widowhood.

A little over two years later, we were preparing to welcome our baby Stephen into our lives. My mother, Nancy, had been to visit us during the last couple months of my pregnancy to attend baby showers and help to make final preparations for the nursery. She was so excited to realize that her oldest child (me) was finally about to give birth to her seventh grandchild! I gave birth to our baby Stephen on June 2, 2000, by C-section. When we got home with our new baby, there was a rather frantic message on our home phone recorder from my sister Carrie. She had intended the message for Ralph before he brought me home from the hospital. Unfortunately, he had not checked the voice mail for a couple days because he was mostly with me at the hospital. Just after we got home from the hospital with Stephen, Ralph left to go to the pharmacy to have prescriptions filled for me. I saw the phone message light flashing and proceeded to push the button to listen to the messages. The very first message from my sister was a message I will never forget. She shared the news that our mom had just been diagnosed with fourth Stage metastatic brain cancer over the weekend. I was devastated and completely heartbroken to hear this news. I fully expected that Mom would be the same loving and doting grandmother to *our baby* that she had been to all of my siblings' children. I sobbed inconsolably and felt that God had made a huge mistake in allowing this to happen. This was the time in my adult life when I needed my mom the most! I could hardly believe that God had allowed this to happen at the time when I was supposed to be rejoicing over the birth of our first child. The fact that mom had developed cancer was not a total shock because she had smoked cigarettes ever since her college days. What *was* a horrible shock was to learn that her cancer was considered terminal.

Just three weeks later, we packed up everything needed for a new baby, and we drove ten hours north to my hometown in New York State to visit Mom and allow her to meet her newest grandchild. She had started radiation treatments in hope that the aggressive cancer could be slowed, but I could tell from looking at her that she was a very sick woman. Our visit was short, but memorable because I knew that she would not last long, according to the physician's grim prognosis. I have a special memory of her bathing Stephen in her kitchen sink, overjoyed to see that we now had a child of our own. She was thrilled that we named our baby Stephen in honor of my younger brother Stephen. She rejoiced with us despite her cancer, and we were so grateful to have these few days with her.

Less than two months later, we received a phone call that we terribly dreaded. Mom was deteriorating rapidly, and my sister asked that we come home as soon as we could get there. Although we left for New York within hours, I cried and pleaded with God to let Mom live until we got to the hospital. God faithfully answered that prayer! She was unable to speak by the time we arrived, but when I placed Stephen in her arms in her hospital bed, she smiled and teared up. I knew that God had kept her alive until she saw us and her precious new grandson.

My siblings and I began a forty-eight-hour vigil during which we played hymns and prayed with mom repeatedly. The nurses said she could still hear us so we continually spoke to her of our love and the fact that she would soon be with Jesus. When Mom took her last breath, we all breathed a sigh of relief that her earthly suffering was ended. Nonetheless, the finality of my first parent's death took a painful toll on my emotions and I grieved very deeply for months and months. My grief was interspersed with the joy of being a new mom—there were days when I would cry and rejoice all in the same hour! During these rough months, Jesus comforted me and eventually healed me of my deep grief, allowing me to focus on being the best mom I could be to our baby. Many expressions of love and sympathy were extended to me during these months and our entire Christian community supported us through faithful and persistent prayer.

Six months after Mom died, Ralph's mother Ruth, was diagnosed with colon cancer that had metastasized to other parts of her body. We were told she would live between three and six months, however, she lived exactly three *weeks*. Saying goodbye to Ralph's mom was in some ways a blessing as she had been diagnosed with Alzheimer's disease a year earlier. She was to the point where she could no longer live safely on her own or be trusted to take her medications properly. At the same time, we felt profound grief once again that she would not get to be a grandmother to Stephen, and we would greatly miss her.

Throughout the loss of our three parents, we learned that God is faithful and that He can be trusted to comfort us in our time of great sorrow. We saw God carry us and sustain us as we walked through the months of grief and heartache. He balanced our grief with the joy of having a son to love and care for. We truly experienced God's comfort and God's healing strength to get through these difficult months. Psalm 147:3 promises: "He heals the brokenhearted and binds up their wounds."

God demonstrated His grace through Christian friends who gladly stepped in and loved our baby as if he were their own grandchild! There were two special families who always included us in their holiday celebrations for Easter, Christmas, and Thanksgiving. Because neither Ralph nor I had any family members living near to us, it meant so much that we were a part of these families' holiday celebrations. God further demonstrated His grace to us through the blessing of a meaningful relationship with my dad and stepmother, Marvella. They loved our children deeply and our children grew up making wonderful memories with them. They were extremely generous toward us, taking us to Disneyland and on two cruises that featured swimming with dolphins, snorkeling, and a day in the huge Atlantis waterpark in the Bahamas. Dad and Marvella celebrated Thanksgiving with us for several consecutive years and we always looked forward to playing card games and checkers with them. Annika came close one time to beating her grandfather at checkers, but he always reigned as the checkers champion in the family.

Many other fun family memories were made when we went to Florida to visit Dad and Marvella. The kids loved boating and fishing trips, miniature golf, and even visits to the country club. I'll never forget when Annika spotted Joe Namath (former NFL football player) in the club's dining room during Easter dinner. Dad took her over to meet him and she couldn't wait to tell Mr. Namath that she had seen him recently on an old episode of The Brady Bunch. She was so excited to have a photo taken with him that she returned home to tell her classmates that she had a picture of the famous Joe Namath standing next to her! Of course, none of her classmates had ever heard of Joe

Namath, so they could not share Annika's zeal over the experience.

When Annika was quite young there was another memorable country club experience that made a lasting impression on all of us. After she finished eating her meal, she leaned back into her chair and proceeded to put her feet up on the table to make herself comfortable. I was horrified and embarrassed and tried to quickly get her feet off the table. However, I was not fast enough. Dad was seated next to Annika and when I looked at his eyes, I immediately spotted his disbelief and displeasure at this disrespectful action. To make matters worse, there were elderly friends of Dad and Marvella seated at the table with us. The entire scene is funny now, but it was not so at the time. The children both knew that their grandparents always expected good manners, but most certainly while dining at the country club! Thankfully, that never happened again while eating out in a restaurant.

Dad enjoyed good health for many years as he aged, but at the age of eighty-five he was diagnosed with throat cancer. He sought and received the best medical care available. Marvella took excellent care of Dad throughout his illness. He endured radiation and chemo treatments and fought the disease bravely, but he died a year later just three months after his eighty-sixth birthday. One thing that stood out to me was his choice to never complain nor display self-pity, no matter how hard things got. For several months he had a feeding tube and ate a liquid diet to sustain him. This had to be so hard for Dad because he loved to eat, and he had always enjoyed taking us to the Japanese steakhouse when we visited together. I cherish all the memories of my father and the things he taught me in life. He was truly a gentleman who connected well with people from all walks of life. He had the gift of hospitality, always welcoming friends, family, and other guests into his presence and home. I am thankful for the legacy my dad left and I will always miss his phone calls, visits, and the great stories he told.

For all our parents, there was comfort in the fact that they knew with certainty they were going to Heaven upon death. Ralph's parents had a deep faith in Jesus Christ that had anchored and guided them throughout Ralph's lifetime. Both my mom's hospital chaplain and my dad's pastor gave me reassurance that each had trusted in Christ for their salvation, although neither had openly expressed much about their spiritual beliefs earlier in life.

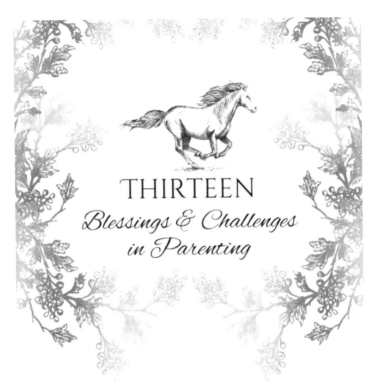

THIRTEEN
Blessings & Challenges in Parenting

We are still humbled, amazed, and deeply grateful to God for allowing us to have and raise two children. We have experienced great joy as we have raised our children to young adulthood. We have also experienced many difficulties, challenges, and heartache along the way. There were times of struggle when we wondered if we were going to make it! Thankfully, our Rescuer God threw us many life savers to encourage us and preserve our sanity throughout the really tough times.

We began our parenting journey determined to follow principles we learned in a parenting class we had taken before Stephen arrived. This class placed an emphasis on getting your baby on a structured feeding and sleep cycle. Although we were not rigid followers of the structure, we were very fortunate in that both children were sleeping through the night within a few weeks of Stephen's birth and Annika's adoption. Surely God knew that we were older parents and not able to function as well without adequate sleep at night! While we enjoyed feeding and rocking our children at bedtime, we were thankful to only have a few weeks of middle-of-the-night feedings.

As babies, both Stephen and Annika responded well to having music played as they went to sleep at night and during daytime naps. We still have a collection of CDs containing baby lullabies or instrumental hymns that were used for several years. Even as the toddler years passed, both kids continued to love having music in their rooms, in the car, and throughout our home. I highly recommend introducing your children to music as soon as they come home from the hospital or their adoption journey.

We took the children to the church nursery as soon as we felt ready to leave them during the worship service. They adjusted well to the nursery experience and did not cry, scream, or throw fits when we left them. Beginning this habit early in their lives helped them get accustomed to being cared for by other responsible adults while we were at the adult worship service. Throughout the children's young years, they attended the age-appropriate worship and Sunday school classes where they were introduced to God, Jesus, and the Bible. Our church did an excellent job teaching about God's love, the Gospel, and the Bible. We read Bible stories to them at home regularly so that a good foundation for knowing God through the Bible was established. When they were old enough to attend church camp, both Stephen and Annika attended and were mentored by staff and other camp counselors who helped them grow in their faith. We were not particularly good at having structured family devotion times; however, each child was hearing about God and Jesus during the hours we spent reading with them one-on-one.

Some of the highlights of our years of parenting young children included memorable vacations. For several years we traveled to Florida or Alabama beach destinations to vacation with another family whose young children were close in age to our children. These trips were filled with happy moments and memories of watching the kids play in the sand and the ocean. What a production it was each morning getting sunscreen on all five of them before heading to the beach! It helped so much when the rash guard shirts became available because that eliminated having to apply sunscreen to backs, shoulders, chests, and arms. Those shirts were wonderful until the kids got older & began rebelling against wearing the rash guards. Mostly we cooked meals in our condo, but we went out at least one evening for seafood at local restaurants. Taking five young kids and four adults out to eat was quite an effort in the early years. Other moments of vacation joy included kite-flying, swimming in the pool, playing games, and reading to the kids prior to bedtime. When the boys got older, they were thrilled to go deep sea fishing or windsurfing. The vacation memories made with our friends are dear to our hearts.

God helped us establish many fun family traditions including trips to a pumpkin farm each fall and a Christmas tree farm every December. Inevitably, the children chose the largest and heaviest pumpkins (which the parents usually had to carry) from the pumpkin field and the largest trees from the Christmas tree farm. For Easter, we often went to Easter egg hunts where our children raced to see who could find the most eggs. Easter mornings we attended worship services and went out to eat with close friends.

On our last family vacation with two teenagers, we traveled to Disneyland for a few days and then went to a beach on the west coast of Florida. The weather was miserably hot and humid during our days at Disney. I was so affected by the heat that I could barely walk from ride to ride without having to find shade in which to rest. Even the kids were very hot, but at least they had the energy to run to each ride to get in the "fast lane" with shorter waiting times. I mainly remember just trying to survive each of the three long, hot and humid days until I could collapse in our air-conditioned room. We could not buy water bottles fast enough on that trip!

After we left Disney, we spent the remaining time of that vacation on the beach. The first night we were there, we attempted to bake a frozen pizza in the oven and the oven filled with smoke. The smoke quickly filled the condo while a small fire in the oven burned up our pizza! Somehow the fire burned itself out soon after we turned off the oven but we were left with smoke that permeated every room in the condo! So much for dinner on our first night.

The next day, we noticed that the air conditioning was not working very well. After calling the maintenance office, we learned that it would be several hours before our unit would receive service.

Because we are not people who spend *all* day on the beach, we really needed our condo to come back to in order to avoid getting sunburned. The kids were very unhappy that we would not have an air-conditioned condo where they could seek refuge from the sun and heat.

The next thing that went wrong really pushed our frustrated children over the edge. As they attempted to go outside to the balcony, the sliding door broke, and the door could not be opened far enough to step outside! That did it—the broken sliding glass door was the last straw and everyone lost confidence that this would be a good vacation and blamed me because of the "cheap" condo that I had picked out! I was so discouraged that I started to cry. Stephen & Annika did not console me but instead said that this was the last time that I would choose the condo. Little did I know that may have been the last vacation for just the four of us. Stephen was unavailable to travel with us the next summer, and Annika requested that one of her friends come with us for the next year's beach vacation.

While there are mostly happy memories of raising our children, we certainly faced challenges in parenting. When we adopted Annika, there were new dynamics in our home that were typical of what you would expect for adoptive families. Thankfully, we had many people praying fervently for us through the especially difficult years.

We believe that God answered those prayers; sustaining us by His grace and helping us to learn to engage in helpful ways when trouble arose. Over time, as we each made efforts to improve our communication and conflict resolution, we experienced much more peace and joyful time together as a family. Our children matured and began to get along better and show respect for each other. We give all the praise and glory to God for the transformation in our family over the last several years. Our kids deeply love one another and seek to do good to one another. Our son recently asked our daughter for forgiveness for his mistakes in her younger years and they experienced reconciliation as never before. The fact that our children are getting along so well humbles us in adoration and gratitude to God for doing what seemed impossible to us years ago.

In fact, they are doing so well together that they often "team up" to tease us and laugh at our mistakes. They have good reason to tease me though. One time when a waiter asked me what I wanted to drink, I said I would like steak and shrimp! My hearing must be going bad. In another incident, a waiter thanked us after he took our order. I thought he said, "God bless you" so I responded, "God bless you too!" The kids howled about my misunderstanding of what the waiter actually said. I don't think I'll ever forget that moment, because they will never quit teasing me and laughing about it.

Ralph gets his share of teasing, also, because of his unwillingness to change his "outdated" wardrobe. The kids love to criticize his devotion to a rigid daily structure and the funny expressions he learned from growing up in the country. The fact that we have learned to laugh together and not take ourselves too seriously makes for a relaxed and joyful home environment.

I am eternally grateful that both of our children have accepted Jesus Christ as their personal Savior. While their salvation occurred early in their adolescent years, they are now demonstrating a whole-hearted commitment to reading the Bible and growing in spiritual maturity. Ralph and I may have planted seeds of faith into their young hearts, but God has faithfully responded to the prayers of *many* people for our children.

In the end, the joys of parenting our children far outweighed the challenging circumstances we encountered along the way. The Lord has always provided the resources needed to help us at each point of our parenting journey. We are eternally grateful for the prayers and support of our many Christian friends and family who have cared for us over the past twenty-three years.

A couple of the Bible verses that have been especially helpful to us in our parenting journey:

Fathers, do not exasperate your children; instead, bring them up in the training and instruction of the Lord.

Ephesians 6:4

Train up a child in the way he should go; even when he is old he will not depart from it.

Proverbs 22:6 (NASB)

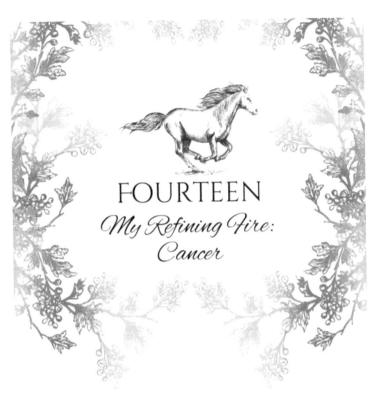

FOURTEEN

My Refining Fire: Cancer

The diagnosis of cancer came on the Monday after Thanksgiving in November of 2021. I had just had two mammograms in August & September of the same year and there was no indication of any abnormality or evidence of breast cancer! I was not totally shocked to learn that I had breast cancer because there was a strong history of breast cancer on my mother's side of the family. In fact, I have spent most of my life in fear of a breast cancer diagnosis. However, I was totally devastated when I learned that I had Stage 3A breast cancer in my left breast. How could this cancer have advanced this far when I recently had *two mammograms* that did not detect any cancer?

Earlier in November I casually mentioned to my OB/GYN doctor that my left nipple looked a little unusual. When I told him my nipple seemed to lay flat or even turned inward, he immediately looked very concerned and advised that I follow up soon with a breast surgeon. He made an appointment for me with a breast surgeon for the following March of 2022. When I came home and told Ralph about the doctor's concern, he was immediately concerned as well and felt that three-to-four months to wait for a follow-up was too long to wait. Years ago, I had seen a well-known breast surgeon in Louisville because I had extra dense breast tissue. We immediately called his office and made an appointment with him for the next week. We were relieved to not have to wait three months or more to see a breast surgeon. I wish I could tell you that I faced this situation with peace and complete trust in the Lord. I was scared, very scared, and I feared the worst.

As soon as the breast surgeon examined my left breast, I could tell by the look on his face that he did not like what he saw on my left breast. In less than ten minutes, he made an appointment for me to have an MRI of both breasts. The MRI was to happen within the next few days. Ralph and I cried out to God, asking that the MRI reveal exactly what we needed to know. We prayed for peace in the face of what might be a serious health crisis for me. The MRI was not too unpleasant of an experience, but the machine was very loud even with the earplugs I was given. We thought it might take a couple days to get the results, but I received a call from the breast surgeon later that very afternoon! The news was not good. My left breast was filled with finger-like projections of cancer. Not only was the cancer scattered throughout my left breast, it had spread into at least two lymph nodes under my left arm. The MRI also revealed that some of the cancer had attached itself to my chest wall behind the left breast. We were relieved to learn that my right breast scan appeared normal.

Several days later, I had a needle biopsy to confirm what the MRI showed and to determine the type of cancer that I had. We learned that my cancer was a lobular type of Her2+ metastatic breast cancer. The cancer had advanced to stage 3A and it was an aggressive type of cancer. My breast surgeon, now specializing in diagnosing breast cancers, had recently given up his surgical practice and he referred us to a general surgeon who performed many mastectomies in her practice. He also referred us to an oncologist and a plastic surgeon.

Late in December, we met with my general surgeon, and we agreed that she would perform the outpatient procedure to implant the port that would be used for my chemotherapy treatments. The standard treatment of care for my type of breast cancer required chemotherapy *first* in order to shrink the cancer, followed by surgery and radiation. We also met with my oncologist who presented us with treatment information and the option to be part of a clinical trial to use less aggressive chemotherapy. After much prayer, we opted to receive the standard and more aggressive treatment.

The Christmas holiday season passed quickly in a blur. All I can remember was that I was very sad about my cancer diagnosis and dreading the upcoming treatments of chemotherapy. While I tried to cover my fear and sadness for the sake of the children, I'm sure they could tell that I was stressed and pre-occupied. My problem-solving attorney husband busied himself by reaching out to medical contacts in his healthcare legal practice to discuss treatment options and professional reputations of the physicians who would provide my care. We were grateful to learn from Ralph's discussions that I would be receiving care from some of the finest cancer care physicians in Louisville. We felt God's care and protection throughout this process. Once again, many people from church and our family were praying for us and reaching out to support us.

In the first week of January 2022, my port was implanted successfully, and I began chemotherapy treatment the next week. While I dreaded chemotherapy, I was eager to begin the process and I hoped and prayed for a full recovery. I sought God eagerly each day and asked Him to give me strength and grace for one day at a time. Over and over again, God met me with answers to my prayers in both little and big ways.

At my first chemo appointment, I was cared for by very kind and compassionate nurses. The entire infusion treatment took between six and seven hours, which included a cooling cap for my head to aid in the protection of my hair follicles. By the time the treatment was over, I was exhausted and by the next day, I was even more exhausted. The morning after my initial treatment, I felt as though I had been hit by a freight train! I could barely get out of bed and get myself downstairs. I had never felt so weak in my life.

And so began the process of chemo infusions over the next five months. For every three-week cycle, I would receive the harshest chemo chemicals on week one, followed by the less harsh drugs for the next two weeks. Almost from the start, I experienced significant nausea which required daily anti-nausea medications to manage it. I lost my sense of taste early in the process and during the weeks of the aggressive infusion drugs, I received IV fluids to prevent dehydration. There were very few foods that tasted good to me because I developed a metallic taste in my mouth. I learned from other chemo patients that I would have to drink from plastic cups and utilize plastic utensils to reduce the awful metallic taste. I had to force myself to drink lots of water to keep myself well-hydrated. Even water tasted terrible unless sipped from a plastic cup and straw. My daily Diet Dr. Peppers were placed on a long-term break because they tasted horrible to me. I threw up constantly, but I was never able to master the art of throwing up gracefully. Certain foods would provoke immediate nausea and even bending over a sink to brush my teeth brought about many episodes of throwing up.

As a further complication, because of COVID, I was not permitted to attend church or have any other contact with the outside world for approximately five months, except for doctor and chemo appointments. It was not terribly hard to be this restricted because most days I was too sick and weak to do anything but sit in a recliner. Because I was so weak, I lost the ability to do my lap swimming which I had been doing three to four days a week. This was a big loss for me because swimming was something I enjoyed very much. I later looked back on my frustration with not being able to swim and concluded that I relied too much on swimming to be part of my identity. I wondered if swimming had become an idol in my life.

Many people encouraged me by saying that I was brave and that I was remaining strong in my faith, trusting God one day at a time. Much of the time that was true. God encouraged me with so many verses from the Bible, including the following:

So do not fear, for I am with you; do not be dismayed, for I am your God. I will strengthen you and help you; I will uphold you with My righteous right hand.

Isaiah 41:10

Do not fear, for I have redeemed you; I have summoned you by name; you are Mine. When you pass through the waters, I will be with you; and when you pass through the rivers, they will not sweep over you. When you walk through the fire, you will not be burned; the flames will not set you ablaze.

Isaiah 43:1-2

The Lord is my light and my salvation—whom shall I fear? The Lord is the stronghold of my life—of whom shall I be afraid?

Psalm 27:1

Truly my soul finds rest in God; my salvation comes from Him. Truly He is my rock and my salvation; He is my fortress, I will never be shaken.

Psalm 62:1-2

May Your unfailing love be my comfort, according to Your promise to Your servant.

Psalm 119:76

Let the morning bring me word of Your unfailing love, for I have put my trust in You.

Psalm 143:8

He heals the brokenhearted and binds up their wounds.

Psalm 147:3

Although these verses provided comfort, I vividly recall one day sitting in the recliner weeping and complaining that God had taken *everything*. I felt that He had taken away everything that brought me enjoyment in life. I could not exercise, go out to lunch with friends, go to church or Bible study in person, I could not drive my car, etc. The loss of my hair was very humbling and difficult for me to accept. Dear friends had given me chemo caps of many styles and colors, but even still, I grieved the loss of my hair. I believe that God was using the loss of all these things I had come to depend upon to teach me that I was to depend on Him alone for my satisfaction in life.

Despite all the sickness and hardships of chemotherapy, there were many glimpses of God's grace and provision for our needs. Our church family prayed constantly, including public prayers by our pastor during several church services. Since I could not attend church, we watched the worship services on-line and were blessed to hear those prayers for us. One special treat was having one of our church's home groups come to our front porch to visit us, pray for us, and sing worship songs in the front yard. Ralph helped me out to the front porch so I could stand and be blessed by these dear friends. I was deeply touched to the point of tears, and I shall never forget this expression of God's love for me.

God provided many other blessings to us on my cancer journey. It was a tremendous blessing during this time that Ralph was largely able to work from home due to the thoughtfulness and compassion of his boss. I could not have made it through these difficult months without Ralph's constant presence and care. He proved himself to be the best caretaker I could have had. Countless times, he helped me in and out of the recliner and up and down the stairs when I was weak and unable to walk steadily. Ralph would cook or order out for any food that I was willing to try to eat. Every day, he laid out my medications and ensured that I took them at the proper time. He was there practically every time I was throwing up to clean up after me. I shall never be able to fully express my gratitude for my precious husband and "nurse."

One friend from my Bible study group set up a "Meal Train" for us to receive home-cooked meals on a regular basis. Many friends signed up to bring us meals so that I did not have to cook (and Ralph did not have to fend for himself). We are grateful to all our friends and even people we did not know for their wonderful provisions of food for us. Other blessings included the visits from my girlfriends who would mask up and come to just sit with me and pray with me during difficult days. I received many greeting cards for months from family, friends, and other caring people.

Many of my friends and family members called or texted me regularly to remind me that I was in their thoughts and prayers. One friend even wrote notes to Ralph to affirm and encourage him in his role as husband and caregiver. I was blessed to receive frequent phone calls from my sisters and brothers who encouraged me (and often helped me to laugh) throughout my illness.

One of the greatest blessings during my cancer treatment was the opportunity to lead my Bible Study Fellowship discussion group online using the Zoom platform. When it became obvious that I could not lead my discussion group in person, each of my group members decided to stick with me and finish the year's study online. Each week I looked forward to the love and support of the women and to study the Bible together just as if we were in person. The Word of God and the presence of Jesus in my life were my sure and steady anchor during this storm in my life. God's Word helped me to find courage to face the unknown and to have strength for the daily battle of feeling so rough physically. And the love and support I received from these ladies meant so very much to me.

Yet another blessing during my cancer was the support of my piano teacher, John, who taught my weekly lessons via FaceTime when I was too sick to visit his studio in person. I have played the piano all my life and my piano lessons brought me great joy. God was faithful to allow me to continue piano lessons throughout my time of illness. My piano teacher and his wife, Lynn, were part of my team of faithful prayer warriors. I am eternally grateful to God for the gift of music He has given me. Throughout out my illness, I was blessed to listen to Christian music and play worship music on my piano. Listening to instrumental hymns on my phone always assured me of God's presence no matter what kind of a day I was having.

After five months of chemotherapy and much prayer, I decided that I would undergo a double mastectomy to eliminate the possibility of the cancer returning to my right breast. This was not an easy decision, but once I made it, I felt great peace about my decision. We met with the plastic surgeon in May prior to surgery to discuss reconstruction options. I elected to have temporary breast implants placed on both sides at the same time as the removal of both breasts. Therefore, both a general surgeon and plastic surgeon would be involved in my surgery scheduled for June 1, 2022.

The night before my surgery, I must confess that I gave way to fear and anxiety. I cried about the loss of my breasts and Ralph comforted and reassured me that my decision to have a double mastectomy was in his opinion, the wisest decision. Never once did he try to influence my decision, but he affirmed me in this difficult decision once I made up my mind. On the day of surgery, I had to get up very early after a restless night's sleep and felt very nauseous and hungry at the same time. When we got to the hospital, I threw up in the bathroom even before I was called back for preparation for surgery!

After three to four hours of surgery, Ralph was notified that everything had gone smoothly. I have very little recall of the first few hours after my surgery, but I do remember that I was very sore even while on the strong pain medication. I was completely bandaged up so that even if I were tempted to look, I was unable to see the surgical site or the temporary implants. Just as well, for it was hard enough to cope with what I saw a few days later when dressings had to be changed.

My dear sister Carrie flew to Louisville on the very day of my hospital discharge to help Ralph take care of me for a few days. She was a tremendous blessing both to me and to Ralph. She took over managing my medications and helping Ralph to measure the output from my drainage tubes. Carrie is a science teacher by profession, and she was so helpful to make a chart as a way to record the drains' output.

She refused to leave my side day or night. I had to sleep in a recliner downstairs for several nights, and she slept on the sofa next to me to help me with late night and early morning medications, get me safely to the bathroom, etc.

When I was able to shower after a few days, it took both Carrie and Ralph to get me into the shower and help me to bathe. It took both of them to dry and lotion my skin and replace the bandages. As it turned out, we really *did* need all the help she provided for the first week after my surgery. Carrie is a wonderful cook as well, and she cooked delicious meals for us during each day she stayed with us. My other siblings (Judy, John, and Steve), and my stepmother, Marvella, were also so kind to call me, send cards and flowers during my recovery time. God provided me His constant reassurance through their love, thoughtfulness, caring words, intercessory prayer, and incredible support. Each person that He sent played a critical role in my healing in their own unique way.

A couple days after surgery we received the wonderful news that the tissue pathology report came back negative for cancer! An MRI before my surgery showed that the cancer had greatly shrunk, but we needed the confirmation of the tissue pathology to fully confirm that I was cancer free. The tissue pathology of my lymph nodes also showed the absence of cancer. God had performed a miracle through the chemotherapy and by His grace, allowed me to be completely healed of cancer! Along with my family, friends, and our children, we wept tears of joy, giving all the praise and glory to our God. He is truly the Great Physician, and I am still humbled to realize that there could have been a much different outcome. I may not know why God chose to heal me of cancer, but I do know that He has brought many blessings from this suffering. God never wastes our suffering and indeed, many good things have already come from my cancer journey. I'm confident that even greater things will be accomplished as I seek to glorify God by sharing my testimony of His faithfulness.

Following surgery, I faced another major decision—whether or not to have radiation treatments. We met with a radiation oncologist who strongly suggested that I have radiation treatment to ensure further protection against the cancer coming back. We also sought a second opinion with a nationally known oncologist who practiced in Indianapolis, Indiana. In her research, she concluded that statistically, there was no benefit to having radiation for someone who was declared cancer-free at time of surgery. We also discussed the many lasting and negative side effects of radiation and whether the possible benefits outweighed the risks or not. From her research and experience, she felt the *risks* of radiation outweighed the possible benefits for someone in my situation. Our only way to make this decision was to pray for the wisdom and guidance of our Heavenly Father. I went back and forth on whether or not to receive the proposed radiation, but after much prayer I came to this conclusion:

If the cancer came back and I had *not* done everything available to prevent a recurrence, I knew that I would be angry with myself. Furthermore, my life was in God's hands, and I trusted that the length of my life was not determined by the decision I made about radiation.

We learned that my "case" would be presented to a tumor board which consisted of oncologists, radiation oncologists and surgeons at the hospital where I had surgery. The board's recommendation was that I have the radiation to minimize the chance of the cancer reoccurring. After all these considerations, Ralph and I decided that I would receive the twenty-five radiation treatments which were to start in early September.

Many people had told me that radiation was the easiest part of cancer treatment, that it was no big deal. I found this not to be the case! It was very difficult to raise and keep my arms in the position required for my treatments. In particular, it was so hard to keep my left arm overhead for the fifteen or so minutes needed for treatment. Both of my shoulders are prone to dislocation, so this was a vulnerable position for my arms to be in. As my skin is fair and very prone to sunburn, the radiation treatments began to severely burn the skin on my chest to the point where I had to stop radiation for a few days. Thankfully the short break and the radiation crème I'd purchased were helpful in calming the redness in my skin so I could resume and complete treatment. I am so grateful that neither shoulder dislocated during treatment, nor do I have permanent scarring from the radiation.

From the time I had surgery in June 2022 until February of 2023, I continued to receive chemotherapy treatments. The drugs used for this phase of treatment did not include the harsh chemo drugs I had received earlier in 2022. During this time my hair began to slowly grow back, and I eventually stopped wearing the chemo caps which had become a daily necessity to cover my bald head. I must say that losing my hair was a difficult part of cancer treatment, but I think being so sick was worse! I did have a wig which I purchased shortly after my diagnosis, but I did not really like how it looked on me and so the only time I wore it was to Annika's high school graduation.

On the last day of my chemo treatment earlier this year, I was ready to celebrate being done and being a cancer survivor. The wonderful nurses who had cared for me insisted that I ring a cowbell to indicate to other patients that I'd made it through my treatments. At first, I was hesitant, because I had met and seen other cancer patients who were probably not going to live. But I decided to ring the cowbell to give hope and encouragement to the many patients in the infusion center that day. It had brought me hope whenever I witnessed a patient ring the bell on their last day of treatment. The nurses also gathered around me in my infusion chair to have a photo taken with all of them. I am happy to have that photo to remind me of the incredible kindness and compassion these nurses showed to me throughout my time in treatment. God's grace in his provision of care for me was particularly evident in the thoughtful care I received from two nurses who shared my faith in God.

At this point in my recovery from cancer, I am doing well, overall. I have nerve pain under my left arm where nerves were severed during surgery and further aggravated by the radiation treatment. We have learned that this is quite common for mastectomy patients. I also deal with fatigue which hits me especially in the early evening after dinner. Often, I will "catnap" in the recliner before heading up to bed between 9:30 and 10:00 p.m.

As I write this chapter, I have every reason to believe that I remain cancer-free. I am continually amazed that many friends, my family, and my church family continue to pray for me. The biggest lesson I learned throughout my journey was the depth of God's faithfulness and that I could trust Him completely. I know and have experienced the deep, abiding love of God throughout my cancer journey. My Redeemer Jesus Christ has restored to me everything *I thought* I lost and brought me more joy than I ever thought possible. I am aware that my days are numbered by the Lord as it says in the Bible. As long as I have breath, I will praise and honor my Lord and Savior. I will go where He asks me to go, and I will serve Him all the days of my life. My sole purpose is to worship Jesus and to share the hope of the Gospel.

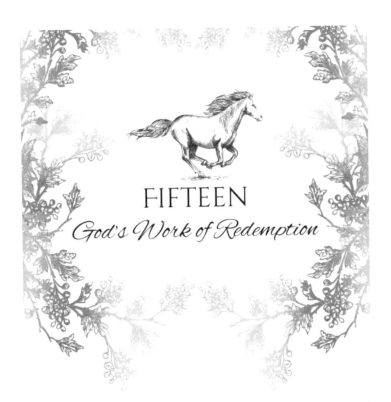

FIFTEEN

God's Work of Redemption

This chapter is dedicated to the Lord's work of redemption and restoration of the brokenness described in previous chapters. In the Bible, there is a passage about God extending hope to the Israelites and a prophecy about a future restoration for the nation of Israel. The prophet Joel wrote in Joel 2:25-26:

I will repay you for the years the locusts have eaten— the great locust and the young locust, the other locusts and the locust swarm—my great army that I sent among you. You will have plenty to eat, until you are full, and you will praise the name of the Lord Your God, who has worked wonders for You; never again will My people be shamed.

God has been more than faithful to restore to me many things which the locusts of my sin and brokenness "ate away" from my life. Indeed, the Lord has "repaid" me with blessings beyond measure. One example of this is what God has done to grant me opportunities to play the piano to serve Him. Earlier in this book I described "piano shame" and the things that contributed to it. Not only has God healed me of this shame, but He has also graciously given me opportunities to play the piano in a variety of settings over the past several years.

One of the first opportunities came when I was invited to accompany a women's Gospel quartet called "Rhythms of Grace." The quartet sang mainly in small churches, often in rural country settings. It was a joy and a privilege to not only rehearse with these four ladies, but also to travel to the churches and perform for their small congregations. On several occasions, I would miss a note here and there, but I was shown nothing but grace from the ladies. Often, I would have to play a piano that was way out of tune or a keyboard that was smaller than the normal eighty-eight keys.

Running out of keys to play was a challenge that would intimidate any pianist!

I distinctly recall the quartet performing at an outdoor women's prison ministry event when the wind whipped up and suddenly *blew* my pages of music off the music stand. The ladies had to stop singing and help me retrieve my scattered music. Needless to say, I was horrified that this had happened. But the prison inmates just smiled and laughed along with us at this unfortunate mishap. And so, we began the song again and completed it before the wind "stole" my music again. After the performance I drove home crying and literally shouted out to the Lord "Why didn't you let me play perfectly?!" In a still small voice, I heard God say to me:

"I didn't call you to play the piano perfectly, I only called you to play."

I dried my tears and felt that this was a moment I would never forget. What a joy to know that I was not expected to play perfectly, but just to do my best regardless of the circumstances. From then on, my music was always in sheet protectors secured in a three-ring binder!

On another occasion when the "Rhythms of Grace" quartet performed outdoors at a women's ministry event, I faced another unexpected challenge. There were bees flying all around my face, making it hard to concentrate on my music. But the worst moment came when one of the bees flew up inside the bottom of my skirt! I could hear and feel it buzzing around but fortunately, it did not sting me before exiting my skirt. Despite the distraction, I somehow managed to keep my place in the music and not mess up the performance. After that event, I told the ladies I did not want to play outdoors ever again! And as I recall, we were never asked to perform outdoors again.

The Rhythms of Grace quartet stayed together for many years, even after two of us had babies which made rehearsals a bit more interesting and challenging. Through my season of accompanying these special ladies, the Lord restored to me the joy of piano playing and I shall always be grateful for this opportunity.

God has given me many other opportunities to use the gift of piano playing over the years. I have played for a variety of churches both for solo piano and being part of a worship band. For several years I played for a local church with their worship band and became good friends with the vocalists and other band members. I loved serving at this special church and will always cherish the friendships I made there.

You might wonder how God could possibly redeem my abortion. After I completed the "Songs of Deliverance" Bible study over twenty years ago, the Lord has called me to share my testimony of His healing power. I have had the opportunity to share my testimony publicly on many different occasions, including at my former church (Southeast Christian), at the annual Right to Life event on the Jefferson County Courthouse steps, and at the annual fund-raising banquet for BsideU for Life, the local pregnancy resource center located in downtown Louisville, Kentucky. While it is never easy to talk about my abortion experience, God has blessed me and allowed me to share boldly about His healing work in my life.

God has given me the privilege of serving with BsideU for Life in many different capacities, including serving as a member of the Board of Directors for six years. I have counseled with many post-abortive women for nearly twenty-five years and continue to serve as a group facilitator for the post-abortion Bible study called "Forgiven and Set Free." As a group facilitator, I have witnessed God heal countless women from the emotional, psychological, and spiritual consequences of their abortions. Working with women of all ages and backgrounds, I have never ceased to be amazed at the healing that the Lord brings to those who turn to Him in humble repentance. Watching God transform hearts and truly deliver women from years of bondage and shame has been one of my greatest joys.

Only God could take such an ugly part of my past and use it to help other women be set free from their abortion wounds. I recently worked through the Forgiven and Set Free Bible study with a woman who lived across the country. We used our computers to connect online for our weekly meetings. This client had been robbed of abundant life for over forty years due to the paralyzing guilt and shame of her abortion. For several weeks, we met on Zoom to study the lessons which were focused on the character of God. My client deeply repented of her sin, grieved the loss of her child, and accepted God's gift of mercy and grace. I watched God transform a spiritually broken woman into a hope-filled Christian who was finally relieved of her burden. At the conclusion of the Bible study, the Lord provided, (through a pro-life ministry), the finances for my client to fly to Louisville, Kentucky for a memorial service for her aborted baby. Our society does not offer the chance to express grief over babies lost to abortion or miscarriage. You may wonder what would be the purpose of having a memorial service for a baby who was aborted so many years ago.

My answer is that the memorial service is a designated time and place for a woman to acknowledge her baby's worth and dignity, provide a safe place to grieve, and hear a pastor's message of forgiveness and hope. While we wept many tears of sorrow during this service, we also celebrated that her child would be there to welcome her into Heaven. God truly performed a healing miracle in my client's soul through the memorial service.

What if *you* have had or participated in an abortion in the past or even recently? I believe that there are thousands of women & men who chose or financed an abortion or were forced by parents (or others) to have an abortion. Many of these individuals have come to deeply regret their abortions and have never known how or where to get help for their spiritual and psychological distress. You may be one of those individuals and you have lived in silence with repressed grief, guilt, and shame over your abortion. You may have suffered with depression that is related to your abortion. Or, you may have been unable to have children and you feel that God may be punishing you for your abortion. Perhaps you feel distant or alienated from God because of your abortion.

There is GOOD NEWS for you. First and foremost, God offers mercy and forgiveness for anyone who comes to Him in repentance. He sent His only Son, the Lord Jesus Christ, to die on the cross in our place (John 3:16). God is holy and He cannot be in the presence of sin (1 Peter 1:16). We have all inherited Adam and Eve's sin nature ever since their fall in the Garden of Eden (Ephesians 2:1, Romans 3:23). Thus, each person must be *reconciled* to God through His son Jesus Christ (Romans 5:10). Jesus's death on the cross satisfied God's wrath over mankind's sin. That is, Christ provided the only acceptable sacrifice for my sin and your sin (Romans 3:24-25). Through belief in His death and resurrection, we are reconciled to God who gives us the gift of eternal life (1 Timothy 1:16). The offer of salvation from sin's punishment is available to all who believe and place their trust in Christ (Acts 4:12).

Secondly, there are pregnancy resource centers in nearly every major city in the U.S. which offer one-on-one counseling for post-abortive women. Many resource centers offer small groups which study the Forgiven and Set Free Bible study (or something similar) as a process for healing abortion scars. In the back of this book, I have listed other resources for helping women (and men) find healing from the guilt and shame of their abortions.

God has further redeemed my life through the ministry of Bible Study Fellowship. Bible Study Fellowship (BSF) is an international ministry with Bible classes meeting all over the world. In every city with a BSF class, the same lesson is studied each week. Each year, a different study of a book or books of the Bible is offered free of charge to participants. BSF participants pay only for the study materials. BSF relies on voluntary contributions to support the extra resources provided on the BSF website and app.

I was introduced to Bible Study Fellowship during the first few months after I married my husband. A lady in our Sunday school class befriended me and invited me to visit her BSF class in Louisville, Kentucky. I was already studying God's Word with a small group of ladies from the church. I declined her invitation, not once, but several times! However, she persisted in extending her invitation to "come and see" what BSF was all about and I finally agreed to attend. I joined her BSF class immediately! Little did I know that God's Word would so profoundly impact my life. Having never studied the Bible in depth, I was amazed at how much there was to learn about God's plan for redemption in sending His only Son Jesus Christ into the world.

For several years I participated in BSF and grew in my knowledge of God's character and trustworthiness. The women in my groups loved God's Word, prayed for one another, and were deeply committed to following Jesus. The year I was pregnant with our son Stephen, I was asked to be a discussion group leader. Becoming a group discussion leader meant I would complete the lesson and attend a leader's meeting to help me be prepared to lead my group on class day. It also meant completing the Homiletics assignment for deeper understanding of the Scriptures covered in each week's lesson. Basically, it meant more preparation and extra responsibility to care and pray for the women assigned to my group. After praying about this decision, I timidly, but joyfully accepted this new role. I had no idea what a blessing it would be to serve as a leader for other women who desired to study the Bible. I have greatly enjoyed all my years of leadership and especially the women God has placed in my groups. Many of my group members have become dear friends and sisters in Christ.

I enjoy leading BSF discussion groups because the women typically come prepared to discuss each week's lesson. The discussions are rich and meaningful because of the different perspective each woman brings to the group. I have found great joy in connecting with the ladies in my group outside of class day through phone calls, meeting for coffee, or sending notes and communicating through text messages. I am so blessed to have many friendships with the other leaders and the ladies in my discussion groups. BSF has enriched my life in more ways than I could have imagined.

I also have had the privilege of serving as a Children's Leader in BSF. This role proved more challenging, because I did not consider myself to be very good at working with children! When I first became a children's leader, we were required to memorize a three to five-minute Bible story to tell the children. This really intimidated me! But that did not matter because I soon learned that God would provide the energy, time, and discipline to memorize Bible stories and learn hymns to teach the children. In this new role, I had to depend completely on God to help me on class day. And He was so faithful to give me a joyful and fun co-leader to work with. We laughed at our mistakes and our inability to carry a tune and the children never knew we'd missed a beat! In addition, as mentioned earlier, God truly used my time as a children's leader to prepare my heart to welcome and love an adopted child.

I have been involved with BSF now for over thirty years. I can honestly say that my faith and trust in Jesus has deepened because of this format of Bible study. Quite honestly, the only normal thing I was able to do during my cancer illness was to continue to lead my BSF discussion group. Staying in BSF really kept me going through the months of chemo sickness.

In an earlier chapter of this book, I described some of the challenging years of parenting our two children. I would like to share a few of the ways God has redeemed those difficult years. We are extremely grateful for the work God has done in our children's lives. We give praise and glory to God that both of our children are doing well in all respects.

Most importantly, both children are Christians who are pursuing their own relationships with God. Our son has graduated with honors from the University of Kentucky and is now serving on staff at Christian Student Fellowship (CSF). CSF is a college ministry on the UK campus that impacted our son significantly during his four years at UK.

Our daughter is a second-year nursing student at Cedarville University in Ohio. She is doing well academically, spiritually, and socially and we feel certain that God led us to the right school for her. While her studies are becoming quite challenging, we are trusting God to help her face the rigors of her nursing major.

When the children were growing up, there were a few years where they did not get along very well. In fact, at one point, there was much strife and conflict in our home. I'm extremely thankful to say that they now love and respect one another very well. My children are finally at the stage where they actually seem to be friends with one another. God has graciously redeemed the difficult years and has brought forth a loving relationship between the two children, as I mentioned earlier.

A final word about redemption and restoration in my current life. God has restored to me the time lost to my battle with cancer. For months when I was too sick to attend our church, I felt that I lost the opportunity to build friendships with other women in the church. And yet, God has seen fit to deepen existing friendships and to bring me several new friends at the same time. I have been delighted to get to know more of the younger women at my church. I am currently serving as a mentor and Biblical counselor to two young ladies who are benefitting from our time together discussing God's Word and its application to our lives. Just when I thought I did not have much to offer the younger generation, the Lord has brought these vibrant Christian women into my life. I value my fellowship with these ladies and the opportunity to pour into their lives with the wisdom God has granted me.

Stephen, June 2022

Annika, October 2023

Our Family, November 2023

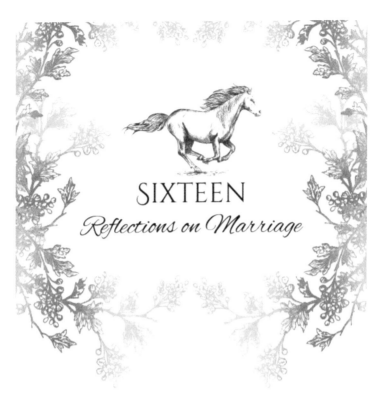

SIXTEEN

Reflections on Marriage

As I reflect on our marriage of thirty-one years, I am deeply grateful for the things that have drawn us together—both times of joy and ease, as well as times of great difficulty and sorrow. I find that the trials of life have done much to mature us as individuals and as a couple.

We married later in life than most people and I remember well the challenges of bringing together two single adults set in their ways. Although Ralph and I loved each other deeply, we had several struggles early in our marriage due to our own sin habits and dysfunctional upbringings. Let's face it—most families have some degree of dysfunction which we carry into our adulthood as well as marriage if not resolved. The challenges and struggles that we experienced were not unusual, but they were somewhat of a surprise and certainly perplexing. We sought the help of other married couples as well as a Christian counselor who came alongside us as we dealt with our issues. We benefitted greatly from the wise counsel of these individuals who encouraged us and pointed us to the Bible for guidance. Over the years, we have developed a healthy and happy marriage which has stood the test of time. We have both matured and grown together as partners in living out the covenant of Christian marriage. We have grown spiritually, both individually and as a couple. We are each other's best friend and are committed deeply to loving each other until we are separated by death.

In the remainder of this chapter, I've noted some key lessons I have learned, in the hope that it helps other married couples and singles. If I had learned more of these lessons myself when I was younger, I would have undoubtedly avoided many mistakes and potentially realized many more blessings.

Six Things I Have Learned About Biblical Marriage

First, I would say that a biblical marriage is one which brings honor and glory to God. Marriage is given by God not for the purpose of making each other happy. God created marriage for one glorious purpose: to illustrate the covenant relationship between the Lord Jesus Christ and His Bride, the Church. Christian marriage is not a contract that can be broken but rather a covenant that is binding, unbreakable, and irrevocable. God designed marriage for companionship, procreation, and for the opportunity to pursue God together.

One thing I learned about marriage is that it is not a fifty-fifty proposition. Biblical marriage takes two people, each willing to invest one hundred percent into the relationship. There is no room for half-hearted commitment to serving and loving your spouse. Each person needs to dedicate their energy and time to meeting the needs of their wife or husband. That is not to say that you must spend every waking moment together. It means that you make a whole-hearted devotion to caring for your spouse and meeting his/her needs as outlined in the Scriptures.

Second, I have learned that Christian marriage must put Christ at the head of the marriage. As each partner grows closer to the Lord, there will be a spiritual intimacy that cannot occur outside the context of a biblical marriage. When we got married, our pastor described marriage as a triangle in which Christ was at the top of the triangle and each partner was at the two sides of the base of a triangle. He said that the closer each spouse got to God, the better marriage you would have. Both Ralph and I have proved this illustration to be true. The more that each of us has grown in spiritual intimacy with God, the more joy we have experienced in our relationship. Each of us has spent years reading the Word of God daily and seeking to know Him through prayer. We have developed the habit of seeking to know God's will for decisions and His guidance for every aspect of our lives. We currently pray together each evening before going to bed. Although we have prayed throughout our years of marriage, there is something special about having a designated time of day devoted to praying together as a couple.

Third, I have learned the importance of *listening* carefully to one another's opinion on certain topics or decisions. We do not rush into major decisions. Instead, we take the time to pray individually and as a couple about important things or decisions. If both of us have peace about how to move forward and believe that God has led us to a particular decision, we move forward and act on what the Lord has revealed to us. If one of us does not have that peace, we continue to pray and seek God's will. I brought into our marriage a struggle with indecisiveness. Often, I will weigh the options that are before me but still have a hard time making a decision. I have learned that when I simply do not know what to do, I lean on Ralph to make the final decision. I am grateful for his leadership and godly wisdom that he brings to our marriage each and every day.

One example of me not being able to decide was when we were purchasing a piano with money I inherited from my mom's estate. We had narrowed down the options to two different pianos from two different stores in town. Although we had prayed much about which piano to buy, I felt guilty about asking that we buy the more expensive one. I told Ralph that I could be happy with the less expensive piano and we proceeded to buy the piano. After leaving that store with the check in the dealer's hands, I came home and stewed and worried about whether we had made the right decision. Secretly in my heart, I still desired to buy the other piano for several reasons, but I could not bring myself to admit this to Ralph. I felt good that we had saved money in purchasing the less expensive piano. Finally, I expressed myself and told my husband that I was having second thoughts. He knows me so well and he could tell that I might rather have bought the Steinway piano. He gladly (for my sake) humbled himself and called the dealer from whom we bought the piano that day and told him our predicament. Thankfully the dealer was extremely understanding and told Ralph that he would tear up our check and cancel the order entirely without fee or repercussion. I wept tears of joy and relief that we were going to buy the beautiful Steinway piano that my heart was set on. On the day our piano was delivered, I wept once again because I knew that my mom would have been so happy for me to have this piano. It just happened to be on her birthday, so I had been thinking of her and missing her all day long. This was a lesson about me learning once again to *submit* to Ralph and let him make the final decision. He later told me that he had known that I had a slight preference for the Steinway piano, but he did not want me to feel pressured to buy the more expensive one. He admitted that he should have insisted that we buy the Steinway piano in the first place! The piano looks beautiful and sounds beautiful and I am so happy to be able to play it for my own enjoyment or for guests in our home.

Fourth, I have learned that a Christian marriage will have *challenges* like any other marriage. We learned early on in our married life that we were not meant to stay in isolation just because we were having conflict. Instead of being fearful of what other people might think, we realized that it was important to find other couples to interact with and share our struggles. We were in a Sunday school class with other young married couples, and we were close friends with two couples in particular. While we would talk about our challenges, these young couples did not have the experience of being married long enough to help us through our difficulties. We intentionally sought help from one of the pastors in our church who was known for his ability to counsel younger couples. He and his wife had been married for over thirty years and we felt comfortable in sharing our struggles with them. Since they had mentored lots of couples, they helped us to realize we were not alone in having conflict. More importantly, they took the time to listen to both of us and they made suggestions that could help us individually and as a couple. This couple prayed for us and that was especially meaningful. We also found another couple who had been married several years longer than we had. This couple had dealt with marital conflict and with God's help, had overcome their difficulties to develop a strong marriage. Meeting with this couple helped us to resolve some of our struggles through practical advice. They helped us not take ourselves too seriously and to concentrate on the positive things about our marriage. My overall lesson is this: be intentional about seeking out older couples who have years of marriage experience and are willing to mentor you. If your church has a marriage mentoring program, sign up for a mentor couple who will encourage and give you godly counsel. Make friends with other couples who affirm and bless your marriage!

Fifth, I have learned that every Christian marriage will need opportunities to *recreate* and have fun together. Life is hard enough, so it is important to be intentional about laughing together and pursuing recreation as a way to de-stress and distract yourselves from the routine of life. We had to learn to do this as a couple. During our year of dating, we did many fun things together because Ralph was creative in planning our dates. I learned over time not to be selfish and only do things I was comfortable with, but to step into Ralph's world and learn to enjoy things such as attending football and basketball games. In turn, he was willing to do things I enjoyed, like going to concerts, hiking, and biking. We found that it was healthy to affirm each other's interests, and, in many cases, we learned to enjoy each other's hobbies.

Many of you are familiar with the Kentucky Derby which is a horse race held in Louisville on the first Saturday of May each year. Through Ralph's employer, we had an invitation to attend the Derby one year and I was excited over the prospect of going to the famous Churchill Downs racetrack. I visited several consignment shops in search of just the right outfit and a hat to go with it. When I found a pretty pink tweed suit and a fancy pink hat in one of the shops, I was smitten. I knew I would enjoy wearing an outfit that cost less than $100 and looked good on me. When the day of the Derby arrived, I was excited to go out to the track and spend time with Ralph's co-workers. The very first thing we did when we arrived was to locate the company tent where all kinds of food were available to the employees who attended the Derby. Ralph and I wandered into the tent, got our plates, and piled them high with delicious food. As we were leaving the tent to go find a table, a man stopped us and asked Ralph which company he worked for. Ralph told them who he worked for and the man abruptly said, "You are in the wrong tent!" There we were with plates full of that company's food and feeling horribly embarrassed that we had made such a big mistake. Not knowing what to do, we apologized profusely and sheepishly left the tent to go find the correct tent! The story is now quite humorous, but oh, how embarrassing in that moment!

Ralph tried hard to be a good sport in doing things that I enjoyed but some of those dates were a disaster. He had never canoed before so I decided that for our first wedding anniversary, we would celebrate by going canoeing on the Blue River in southern Indiana. It was an extremely hot day on our anniversary, but we had made reservations, and I was determined to keep them. We checked in and got our life jackets fitted and headed to the van which took us to the drop-in point on the river. Since I knew how to canoe, we decided that I would be in the back seat to steer the canoe. Ralph's job was simply to sit in the front seat of the canoe and take turns paddling on each side. We started out having problems right from our launch from the side of the river because Ralph paddled very hard and made it difficult to point the canoe forward. I gently asked him to paddle less aggressively, and he cooperated. Just when we were getting the hang of working together to keep the canoe going straight, we encountered an unexpected problem. The creek bed ran dry in lots of places which caused us to have to stop, get out of the canoe and lift it over rocks to walk until there was sufficient water to float again. I had no idea that the water level was so low that we'd have to frequently pick up the canoe and walk it yards until we could get in enough water to float! This was an unexpected hassle, and I could tell Ralph was getting hot and frustrated. It wasn't so much that the canoe was heavy, but it was quite tricky not to twist your ankle while carrying it and carefully climbing over the rocks at the same time. This went on for several hours and I could tell that Ralph did not like this adventure. To make matters worse, the mosquitoes were in great population as we headed down the river. Of course, I had not remembered to bring mosquito repellant, so we were constantly batting mosquitoes away from our faces and bodies.

I soon realized that I should have booked the *half-day trip* instead of the full-day trip on the river. By the time we got to the pick-up point downriver, we were both miserable. Ralph tried to hide his frustration, but he was not very successful in doing so. Then we faced a terribly hot ride back to our cars with no air conditioning in the van. I bet you can guess that by now, there was not much conversation between us. I knew I had made an unfortunate choice for how to spend our first anniversary. Needless to say, we never went canoeing on the Blue River again. Thankfully we learned that Ralph liked hiking, and so we did do quite a bit of that before our first child came along.

The sixth thing I have learned about biblical marriage is that the principles outlined in the Bible are *the only* foundation for a thriving and healthy marriage. God's Word is full of wisdom and direction for both husbands and wives. I have learned, often the hard way, that the Bible's teaching on marriage is *the* most important building block for a biblical marriage. That is why it is so important that each partner read and meditate on what the Bible has to share about marriage. I realize that many reading this book will think that is not necessary to know what God says about marriage. But I can tell you that our marriage has survived many difficulties because we knew and obeyed the principles and commands outlined in Scripture. I realize that some think the Bible is outdated and has no relevance in today's society. But this is a grave mistake. You cannot simply have a good marriage by just working on your own to become a better spouse. In fact, if you are not yet a Christian, you will have a less satisfying marriage and, in many cases, you will experience heartache and disappointment.

A few of the Bible verses that have helped us greatly in our roles as husband and wife are:

And though a man might prevail against one who is alone, two will withstand him—a three-fold cord is not quickly broken.

Ecclesiastes 4:12 ESV

In your anger do not sin. Do not let the sun go down while you are still angry.

Ephesians 4:26

Likewise, husbands, live with your wives in an understanding way, showing honor to the woman as the weaker vessel, since they are heirs with you of the grace of life, so that your prayers may not be hindered.

1 Peter 3:7 ESV

Wives, submit to your husbands as is fitting in the Lord. Husbands, love your wives, and do not be harsh with them.

Colossians 3:18-19 ESV

Above all, keep on loving one another earnestly, since love covers a multitude of sins.

1 Peter 4:8

What therefore God has joined together, let not man separate.

Mark 10:9

Rejoice in the Lord always; again I will say, rejoice.

Philippians 4:4

Four Lessons on Building a Christ-Centered Marriage

Early in our marriage, we both recognized the importance of following Genesis 2:24 which states, "For this reason, a man will leave his father and mother and be united to his wife and they will become one flesh."

This is actually a command from God, and it is absolutely required so that a couple can create a new family unit. The goal of this command is for husbands and wives to form an inseparable, "one flesh" bond. This does not mean that a newly married couple does not engage at all with extended family. It just means that the marriage should take priority over all other family relationships. We did not always handle this well due to extenuating circumstances with both of our families. I remember vividly the day I called my mother to "report" a conflict that we'd had and to get her advice on the matter. Although she listened patiently, she offered no real suggestions or advice to me.

Instead, she urged me to reconcile with Ralph and work together to find a resolution to the issue.

Another circumstance we faced was the fact that Ralph's parents were aging and in need of support on a variety of fronts. They were accustomed to seeing him each Sunday for lunch after church and this tradition continued even after we were married. After a few months of this established pattern, I began to grow angry that we had to spend every Sunday driving to meet his parents for an extended lunch. Instead of handling my frustration in a godly, kind way, I began demanding that the weekly tradition be stopped. This placed Ralph in a tough spot as he was an only child and thus, the only caregiver for his parents. Eventually we reconciled the issue by telling his parents that we sometimes needed to just spend time together as a couple. We finally reached a compromise that occasionally allowed us to have our Sunday afternoons together as a couple. We learned that "leaving and cleaving" was important but not always easy to implement.

The second key thing I learned in marriage was the need to forgive and reconcile *quickly* when we had an argument. I brought into our marriage a habit of hanging on to offenses and holding a grudge. Biblical forgiveness was not something I had seen expressed in my family of origin. I do not offer this as an excuse. There was no excuse for the spirit of resentment which I held toward my husband. I sinned in this way greatly, although Ralph was very forgiving toward me. I am learning to not be so easily offended or hurt, but when I am tempted to remain angry, I remember the pain of the years when I allowed bitterness to reign. We thank the Lord for teaching us to handle and resolve conflict when it does arise. In building a Christ-centered marriage, there is no room for grudge-holding or resentment. 1 John 1:9 says, "If we confess our sins, He is faithful and just to forgive us our sins and to cleanse us from all unrighteousness" (ESV). The importance of confession and forgiveness cannot be overstated. We love each other too much to let Satan destroy our oneness with each other or interfere with our peace with Christ.

The third key thing I have learned in building a Christ-centered marriage is the importance of my *individual* relationship with Jesus Christ. To the extent I consistently devote myself to honoring and worshipping Him, is the extent to which I will have peace and stability in my marriage. As expressed earlier, the closer that each partner gets to God, the more joy and intimacy you will have in your marriage. My daily devotion time consists of reading a good devotion book, reading the Bible, and time spent in prayer.

When I skip or miss my time with the Lord, I have found that I may be grouchy or short with Ralph. When I let my heart be filled with and transformed by the love of Christ, I am less tempted to expect Ralph to meet all my needs. In fact, it was not God's intention that our spouses meet all of our needs. I have learned to take refuge in Christ so that when the strong storm winds blow, I won't overly burden Ralph with my emotional and relational needs. I have learned that God is my rock, my fortress and my deliverer (Psalm 18:2).

The fourth key thing I have learned is the importance of praying together as a couple. We have sought to pray together on a regular, if not daily basis. "The prayer of a righteous person has great power as it is working" (James 5:16, ESV). Over the years of our marriage, the power of prayer has strengthened us both individually and as a couple. There is something deeply moving about hearing your spouse pray out loud for your needs. We have seen God answer many, many prayers for us through our years together. God has given us wisdom for major life decisions, for parenting, finances, relationships with friends, and healing from illness. He has been faithful to guide us in choosing the right local church in which to worship.

Five "Best Practices" for Young People

The first bit of advice I have for young women and men who are dating and hoping to marry is to date only Christians. There will be far less struggles, stress, and frustration when you marry someone who shares your Christian values and beliefs. Being unequally yoked is the recipe for confusion, chaos, and possible divorce down the road. The Bible explicitly warns in 2 Corinthians 6:14 "Do not be yoked with unbelievers. For what do righteousness and wickedness have in common? Or what fellowship can light have with darkness?" This is much more than a practical matter—it is a matter of sound Biblical theology designed to protect the believer from heartache, conflict, and disappointment. God knows what is truly for our best, so do not settle for less.

The second "best practice" I would suggest is to avoid sexual temptation in all regards. While it is natural for there to be physical attraction, please recognize that God forbids sex outside the covenant of marriage. Ralph and I were certainly attracted to each other physically while we were dating, but we honored the Lord's command to abstain from sexual relations. Was it difficult to do? Yes, but it was so worth it once we were married and could enjoy God's gift of sex within the context of Christian marriage. The gift of sexual purity is the greatest gift you can give to your future spouse.

I suggest as a third best practice that you *not live together* prior to marriage. An obvious reason is that it goes against God's plan for healthy dating, and it will inevitably lead to sexual involvement. It is not wise to view living together as a "trying out" to see how compatible you are as a couple. Many, if not most couples in our day see nothing wrong with living together to save money or simply for the convenience of it. But living together prior to marriage is a way to enjoy all the benefits of marriage without having to make a long-term commitment to the relationship. You do not need to spend all your waking moments with the person who may be your future spouse. I have known couples who have lived together for years before their marriage, and it has had no positive impact on the outcome. There is ample research which shows that the divorce rate is actually higher for couples who live together before marriage than for those who did not live together. Living together often leads the couple to expect that your spouse can and should meet all your needs. This kind of dependency is wrong because your spouse was never intended to meet all your needs. First and foremost, each partner must be seeking God—for only He can meet all of our needs. It is too much to expect that your spouse become your "all in all." Depending on God will help you not to become overly dependent on your spouse to meet all your needs.

A fourth best practice for a young couple preparing to marry is to receive Christian pre-marital counseling. My church is in the process of establishing a pre-marital counseling program for engaged couples which will be administered primarily by trained lay counselors in the church. Seeking godly counsel will encourage a couple to have conversations about handling money, raising children, and conflict management among others. It is also wise to recognize and understand the impact of differences in upbringing and family of origin patterns and issues. Investing in a few sessions with a certified counselor who specializes in pre-marital counseling will reap benefits once you are married and those differences naturally arise.

A fifth best practice I would recommend is to get to know one another's family prior to marriage. Even though you may see things you do not like, it is better to know what to expect going into your marriage than to be greatly surprised after marriage.

Some of you may ask the question "How long shall we date before getting married?" While I cannot recommend a specific length of time, I believe that one or two years of dating should be sufficient to truly know if you are prepared to commit to a lifetime relationship. Of course, there are extenuating circumstances that may require you to wait for a longer time period. However, I have learned from personal experience that a very long (several years) dating relationship without a commitment to marry is not healthy. Ask God to give you wisdom and discernment throughout your dating relationship and expect Him to show you whether or not this person should become your spouse. The Bible promises "If any of you lacks wisdom, you should ask God, who gives generously to all without finding fault, and it will be given to you" (James 1:5).

As I reflect on these lessons and best practices, I want to emphasize that we are still learning about one another and growing in our ability to love and nurture each other. I remain extremely grateful for God's mercy, wisdom and grace that has been extended to us along the way. We are still a "work in process" and we continue to lean on the Lord Jesus Christ to navigate the challenge of living with an imperfect spouse. I am so thankful for all the Lord has done to deepen our relationship as we have sought to build our lives on the solid foundation of His Word. God's faithfulness has helped us in too many ways to recount. We desire to praise and honor the Lord all the days of our lives.

As Ralph approaches the next season of his life (retirement), we have many hopes and dreams for our future together. We hope that we will be able to travel to points of mutual interest. We hope to spend more time with extended family and friends. We trust that we will live to see Stephen and Annika marry, settle in their careers, and have children of their own. We would be delighted to become grandparents and pour into the next generation. We want our legacy of faith to be passed along to any grandchildren the Lord may give us. We look forward to serving the Lord together and to mentoring young people and couples in our church. We very much pray that God will give us good health and mental stability to pursue all these things!

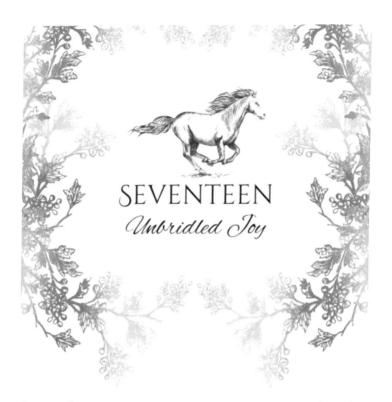

SEVENTEEN
Unbridled Joy

Throughout my story, I have sought to describe how I have been set free from captivity to sorrow, and rescued from sin, shame, guilt, depression and unforgiveness. I truly have found freedom and wholeness through the healing and redeeming work of God in my life. I hope my life story has been an encouragement and inspiration to my readers.

You may think this is the end of my story, but it is really just the beginning. Each and every day I wake up, I'm aware that I have been rescued for a great purpose. I believe that my purpose is to live out my days on Earth serving my Lord and giving Him glory, worship, and honor. I know that every day is a fresh start and an opportunity to do the things He has called me to do. One of those things is to testify to God's goodness and mercy.

As you have read, I pursued many ways of satisfying the "thirst" in my soul for meaning and purpose. I thought I could find my meaning in life through performing well to please other people. I thought that if only I were married, I would be satisfied deep within. For years, I tried to find my identity in my work and career. I craved friendships as a means to satisfy the longing in my soul. I have searched for significance in many ways and things such as materialism, ease of life, pleasure, hobbies, affirmation, and acceptance by others. Even as a wife and mother, I have taken great delight in the lives and accomplishments of my children. While there is nothing inherently wrong with these things, I was never meant to place my hope and identity in these things or people. Earthly pleasures only temporarily quench the thirst that exists in every human soul. Even when we think we have everything we need, there is only emptiness apart from a relationship with Jesus Christ.

This is hard for many people to acknowledge or admit. Most of us do not like to think that we are sinners in need of a Savior. I recently was reading the well-known story of the woman at the well in the Bible. In the book of John, in chapter four, there was a woman whom Jesus approached in the town of Samaria. It was surprising that Jesus would even go through the area, because Jews did not associate with Samaritan people in that day. But Jesus intentionally came to a well in Samaria to find water to quench his thirst. He knew that there was a woman who had sinned sexually with men in her past and was currently living with a man to whom she was not married. This woman likely felt hopeless and downcast because of her sin and shame. Jesus saw her wounded heart and the unsatisfied thirst deep in her soul. He was more concerned about her *spiritual* thirst than His own thirst for physical water.

When she approached the well, Jesus asked her for a drink of water. He knew that this woman had tried to quench the thirst in her soul repeatedly through inappropriate relationships with men. In the course of His conversation with the woman, Jesus offered the woman "living water" so she would not have to return to the well over and over again.

Most people would be like the woman (as I once was) and not even recognize they had a deep spiritual thirst. We do not realize that Jesus knows us intimately and He knows our deepest thoughts, motives, and sin. And yet with patience and great love, Jesus began to explain that *He* was the source of living water. Only Jesus can give the satisfying gift of God's living water to those who ask.

Jesus knew that the woman was pouring her hope into a broken cistern. While the woman did not fully understand that the "living water" was the gift of the Holy Spirit, she asked Jesus to give her this living water. When Jesus asked her to "Go and call your husband," He was gently exposing her sin. She admitted that she had no husband—something she had tried to hide from Jesus. But the Lord knows about our sin and our hurt, and He lovingly draws us to Himself to give us the gift of eternal life. Jesus knows the worst about us, but He wants to give us the gift of salvation despite our failings. He knows our rebellion against Him but loves us and shows us great compassion even while we are sinners.

Like this woman, all people are broken by sin and are in need of redemption. The Lord Jesus has redeemed us from slavery to sin through shedding His own blood at the cross. Our right response to Christ's atoning sacrifice of his life should be to humbly repent of our sin and come to Jesus for forgiveness of our sin. When we make this choice, we receive the indwelling of the Holy Spirit and are born again spiritually. At the very moment we accept Christ as our Savior, we become Christ's *treasured possession* according to Deuteronomy 7:6:

For you are a people holy to the Lord your God. The Lord your God has chosen you to be a people for His treasured possession, out of all the peoples who are on the face of the earth.

Those who believe in Christ and His atoning sacrifice begin a new life filled with inner joy even amid difficult circumstances. We are given the gift of eternal life, and we are redeemed from our empty lives. Just as the woman at the well found a new life of joy, we too will experience deep satisfaction in our souls as we receive the love and mercy of Jesus and seek to follow Him.

The story of the woman at the well ends with her telling others about her encounter with Christ. Many of the townspeople were amazed and were led to seek Jesus for themselves.

Think for a moment about your own life. Do you long for an inner sense of peace and joy in knowing that your sin has been paid for? How are you still trying to satisfy the thirst in your soul? Are you tired of trying to find contentment in the things of this world? Do you know for certain where you will spend eternity?

Jesus answered, "Everyone who drinks this water will be thirsty again, but whoever drinks the water I give them will never thirst. Indeed, the water I give them will become in them a spring of water welling up to eternal life."

John 4:13-14

I know for certain that my sin has been paid for and that I am adopted into God's forever family. Because I have placed my faith in Jesus Christ, I have found a freedom I have never known earlier in my life. I have been set free from slavery to sin and from the power that sin had over me. Knowing that my sins are paid for, I have the freedom to enter into the presence of God. I have freedom from paralyzing fear and anxiety. I have laid down my heavy burdens of guilt and shame. Because I have repented of my sin, I have been set free from the condemnation or punishment by God. I have found freedom from trying to be perfect or constantly seeking the approval of others. I have the freedom to serve God in whatever capacity He calls me. I also have the freedom to refuse to listen to Satan's lies intended to trap me or deceive me. I have been set free from bitterness and with God's help I can forgive others and trust God for justice.

Most importantly, I have inner peace and joy regardless of what happens to me during the rest of my days on Earth. I have been blessed with the gift of contentment. I know that one day, Jesus will call me home to spend eternity with Him in Heaven. I look forward to that day when all earthly sorrows and suffering will pass away. My days will be spent in the presence of the glorious King who has rescued and redeemed me!

Friends, I encourage you to read and meditate upon God's words in the Bible. The truth about God is revealed to us as we read and obey God's Word. The Bible is full of God's promises to His people. We find strength and encouragement as we believe that God is who He says He is and that He does exactly what He says He will do.

I hope that this memoir has been meaningful to you wherever you are in your spiritual journey. I pray for those of you who do not yet have a personal relationship with Christ, that you will seek and come to know Him as your Lord and Savior. I also pray for those of you who have received Jesus as your Lord and

Savior. I pray that you too, will experience the "unbridled joy" of being an adopted and treasured child of God.

I leave you with one of my favorite verses in the Bible:

Delight yourselves in the Lord, and He will give you the desires of your heart.

Psalm 37:4 NASB

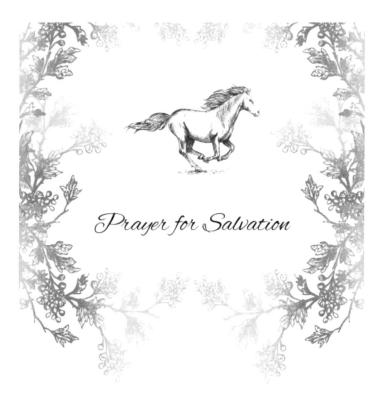

Prayer for Salvation

If you are ready to accept the Lordship of Jesus and submit your heart to Him, I invite you to pray this short prayer:

Dear Lord,

I confess that I am a sinner. I have rebelled against your Word through my thoughts, words, and actions. I humbly turn to You in repentance over my sin. I am sorry for the many ways I have offended You. I choose to put away my sinful ways and turn my life over to

You. I want to live in accordance with Your Word and submit to Your authority to direct my life. Thank You for sending Your Son Jesus Christ as an atoning sacrifice for my sins and I accept Him now as my Lord and my Savior.

Whoever believes in the Son has eternal life, but whoever rejects the Son will not see life, for God's wrath remains on them.

John 3:36

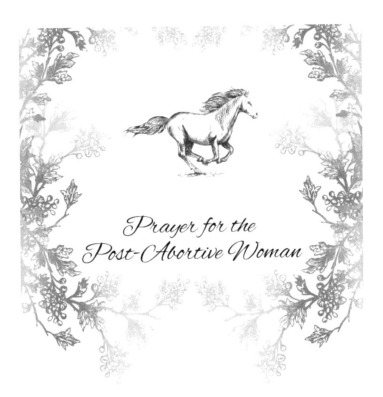

Prayer for the Post-Abortive Woman

If, like me, you have experienced the trauma of abortion, I invite you to pray this prayer for healing:

Dear Lord,

I acknowledge that I have disregarded Your Word by choosing to take the life of my unborn child. I have sinned greatly against You and my child by this selfish act. I come to You in repentance over my sin and I humbly ask for Your forgiveness and mercy. I acknowledge that life begins at conception, regardless of what I knew or thought at the time of my abortion. I know that You are a forgiving God whose mercies are new every morning. Thank You for allowing the sacrifice of Your Son, Jesus Christ, to atone for my sin. Thank You for Your promise to mend the broken-hearted and set free those who are captive in their sin and guilt. My hope is in You alone, for only You can restore the joy of my salvation.

Therefore, my friends, I want you to know that through Jesus the forgiveness of sins is proclaimed to you.

Acts 13:38

Lord my God, I called to You for help, and You healed me.

Psalm 30:2

Set me free from my prison that I may praise Your name.

Psalm 142:7

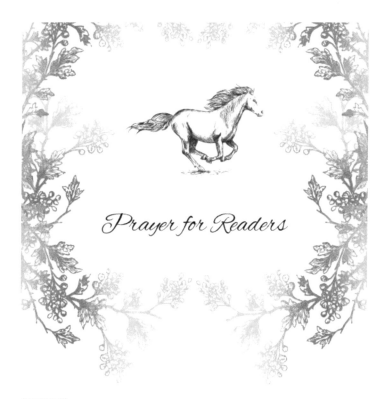

Prayer for Readers

Thank you for reading the testimony of what God has done in my life. I invite all readers to receive this short prayer, reflecting of the desire of my heart for you:

Dear Lord Jesus,

I pray that many people who read this book will place their trust in Jesus Christ as their Lord and Savior. I pray that You will release from captivity those who struggle with shame and guilt. I ask that You would cause my readers to identify the places in their lives where they have not fully received Your forgiveness. Please assure every reader that your atoning death on the cross covers any and all sins.

Thank You for the mercy and grace that You freely offer to those who will believe in You. Thank You that You are God, our Healer, Redeemer, and Rescuer who came to free us to enjoy unbridled joy for all eternity.

Turn to Me and be saved, all you ends of the earth, for I am God and there is no other.

Isaiah 45:22

Even to your old age and gray hairs I am He, I am He who will sustain you. I have made you and I will carry you; I will sustain you and I will rescue you.

Isaiah 46:4

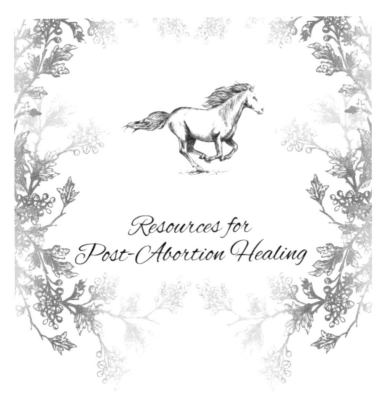

Resources for Post-Abortion Healing

1. Care Net www.care-net.org
2. Focus on The Family www.focusonthefamily.com
3. Rachel's Vineyard www.rachelsvineyard.org
4. *The Unspoken Pain of Abortion* by Teresa Burke
5. *My Father Will Kill Me, My Mother Will Die* by Joan E. Boydell
6. *Surrendering the Secret* by Patricia Layton
7. *Her Choice to Heal* by Sydna Masse & Joan Phillips
8. *You're Not Alone: Healing Through God's Grace After Abortion* by Jennifer O'Neill
9. *Forgiven and Set Free* (Bible Study) by Linda Cochran
10. *Healing a Father's Heart* (Bible Study) by Linda

Cochrane & Kathy Jones

11. *Worthy of Love* (Journal/Bible Study) by Shadia Hrichi
12. *Reclaiming Fatherhood: A Bible Study for Men Seeking Healing After Abortion* by Jill Marquis, Guy Condon, and David Hazard (Care Net)
13. *Helping Women Recover from Abortion* by Nancy Michels

About the Author: Cathy Wilson

Cathy Wilson lives in Louisville, Kentucky, with her husband Ralph. Cathy was born in Olean, New York. She has two sisters and two brothers and was raised by her parents, William and Nancy. Cathy graduated from Olean High School in 1976 and she received a B.A. degree in Biology from Bucknell University in 1980. Cathy earned a Master of Education degree in Counseling Psychology from the University of Louisville in 1994. Cathy married her husband Ralph in

July 1992, and they have two adult children, Stephen and Annika.

Cathy worked as a Quality Assurance Manager within the PepsiCo system, both with Frito-Lay, Inc. and Kentucky Fried Chicken. Cathy has served as a Quality Assurance consultant for numerous corporations and small businesses. For the last thirty years, Cathy has been both a participant and a discussion group leader in Bible Study Fellowship International. Cathy has served in the past on the Board of Directors for BsideU for Life, a pregnancy care center in Louisville, Kentucky. She has also served at BsideU for Life as a facilitator of post-abortion Bible studies. Cathy currently serves as a volunteer counselor and mentor for young women, and a worship pianist at Third Avenue Baptist Church, in Louisville, where she and Ralph are members.

Cathy enjoys lap swimming and is usually found in lane two at the local YMCA! Her hobbies include sewing/making quilts, reading, piano playing, and hiking or walking with her husband and friends. Cathy is known for her gift of encouragement and her devotion to family and many friends.

Connect with Cathy:
cathyspeakslife@gmail.com

Additional copies of this book
may be purchased
on Amazon.com

Made in the USA
Columbia, SC
15 July 2024

38435793R00124